Frances Harper

Frances Harper

Poems, Prose and Sketches

Frances Ellen
Watkins Harper

MINT EDITIONS

Frances Harper: Poems, Prose and Sketches includes poems and prose first published between 1845 and 1894.

This edition published by Mint Editions 2021.

ISBN 9781513290478 | E-ISBN 9781513293325

Published by Mint Editions®

 MINT
EDITIONS

minteditionbooks.com

Publishing Director: Jennifer Newens
Design & Production: Rachel Lopez Metzger
Project Manager: Micaela Clark
Typesetting: Westchester Publishing Services

Contents

A Note from the Publisher

This collection of work follows Miss Frances Harper from her first known publication, *Forest Leaves*, to her last, *The Martyr of Alabama and Other Poems*.

You may find that some poems occur more than once in this book with slight differences, and these have been left unedited so that the reader may see the progression of the poet through time.

M.Clark
Berkeley, CA
2021

Preface

Of the colored population of the United States, three millions are doomed to the horrible condition of chattel slavery. That condition is the annihilation of manhood, the extinction of genius, the burial of mind. In it, therefore, there can be no progress on the part of its victims; what they are capable of being and doing can only be a matter of supposition. It is unlawful to teach them the alphabet; they not only have no literature, but they know not the meaning of the word; for them there is no hope, and therefore no incentive to a higher development; in one word, they are property to be owned, not persons to be protected.

There are half a million free colored persons in our country. These are not admitted to equal rights and privileges with the whites. As a body, their means of education are extremely limited; they are opposed on every hand; they are confined to the performance of the most menial acts; consequently, it is not surprising that their intellectual, moral and social advancement is not more rapid. Nay, is it surprising, in view of the injustice meted out to them, that they have done so well. Many bright examples of intelligence, talent, genius and piety might be cited among their ranks, and these are constantly multiplying.

Every indication of ability, on the part of any of their number, is deserving of special encouragement. Whatever is attempted, in poetry or prose, in art or science, in professional or mechanical life, should be viewed with a friendly eye, and criticized in a lenient spirit. To measure them by the same standard as we measure the productions of the favored white inhabitants of the land would be manifestly unjust. The varying circumstances and conditions of life are to be taken strictly into account.

Hence, in reviewing the following Poems, the critic will remember that they are written by one young in years, and identified in complexion and destiny with a depressed and outcast race, and who had to contend with a thousand disadvantages from earliest life. They certainly are very creditable to her, both in a literary and moral point of view, and indicate the possession of a talent, which, if carefully cultivated and properly encouraged, cannot fail to secure herself a poetic reputation, and to deepen the interest already so extensively felt in the liberation and enfranchisement of the entire colored race Though Miss Watkins has never been a slave, she has always resided in a slave State—Baltimore being her native city. A specimen of her prose writings in also appended. A few slight alterations excepted, the work is entirely her own.

W. L. G.
Boston,
August 15, 1854

FOREST LEAVES

ETHIOPIA

Yes, Ethiopia, yet shall stretch
Her bleeding hands abroad,
Her cry of agony shall reach
The burning throne of God.

The tyrant's yoke from off her neck,
His fetters from her soul,
The mighty hand of God shall break,
And spurn their vile control.

Redeem'd from dust and freed from chains
Her sons shall lift their eyes,
From cloud capt hills and verdant plains
Shall shouts of triumph rise.

Upon her dark despairing brow
Shall play a smile of peace,
For God hath bent unto her woe
And bade her sorrows cease.

'Neath sheltering vines and stately palms,
Shall laughing children play,
And aged sires with joyous psalms,
Shall gladden every day.

Secure by night, and blest by day
Shall pass her happy hours,
Nor human tigers hunt for prey
Within her peaceful bowers.

Then Ethiopia, stretch, Oh stretch
Thy bleeding hands abroad,
Thy cry of agony shall reach
And find redress from God.

The Soul

Bring forth the balance, let the weights be gold,
We'd know the worth of a deathless soul;
Bring rubies and jems from every mine,
With the wealth of ocean, land and clime.

Bring the joys of the glad green earth,
Its playful smiles and careless mirth;
The dews of youth, and flushes of health,
Bring! Oh bring! the wide world's wealth.

Bring the rich radiant gems of thought
From the mines and deeps of knowledge brought;
Bring glowing words and ponderous lore,
Search heaven and earth's arcana o'er.

Bring the fairest, brightest rolls of fame,
Unwritten with a deed of guilt or shame;
Bring honor's guerdon, and victory's crown,
Robes of pride, and laurels of renown.

We've brought the wealth of every mine,
We've ransack'd ocean, land clime,
And caught the joyous smiles away
From the prattling babe to the sire grey.

We've brought the names of the noble dead
With those who in their footsteps tread;
Here are wreaths of pride and gems of thought
From the battle field and study brought.

Heap high the gems, pile up the gold,
Heavy's the weight of a deathless soul;
Make room for all the wealth of earth,
Its honors, joys, and careless mirth.

Leave me a niche for the rolls of fame
For precious indeed is a spotless name,
For the wreaths, the robes and gems of thought,
Let an empty place in the scale be sought.

With care we've adjusted balance and scale,
Futile our efforts we've seen them fail;
Lighter than dust is the wealth of earth
Weigh'd in the scales with immortal worth.

Could we drag the sun from its golden car
To lay in this balance with ev'ry star,
T'would darken the day and obscure the night,
But the weight of the balance would still be light.

"He Knoweth Not That the Dead Are There"

In yonder halls reclining
Are forms surpassing fair,
And brilliant lights are shining,
But, Oh! the dead are there.

There's music, song and dance,
There is banishment of care,
And mirth in every glance,
But still the dead are there.

Like the asp's seductive venom
Hid 'neath flowerets fair,
This charnal house concealeth
The dead that slumber there.

'Neath that flow of song and laughter
Runs the current of despair,
But the simple sons of pleasure
Know not the dead are there.

They'll shudder, start and tremble,
They'll weep in wild despair,
When the solemn truth breaks on them
That the dead, the dead are there.

They who've scoff'd at ev'ry warning,
Who've turn'd from ev'ry prayer,
Shall learn in bitter anguish
That the dead, the dead are there.

FRANCES ELLEN WATKINS HARPER

THAT BLESSED HOPE

Oh touch it not that hope so blest
Which cheers the fainting heart,
And points it to the coming rest
Where sorrow has no part.

Tear from heart each worldly prop,
Unbind each earthly string;
But to this blest and glorious hope,
Oh let my spirit cling.

It cheer'd amid the days of old
Each holy patriarch's breast,
It was an anchor to their souls,
Upon it let me rest.

When wand'ring in the dens and caves,
In goat and sheep skins drest,
Apeel'd and scatter'd people learn'd
To know this hope was blest.

Help me to love this blessed hope;
My heart's a fragile thing;
Will you not nerve and bear it up
Around this hope to cling.

Help amid this world of strife
To long for Christ to reign,
That when he brings the crown of life
I may that crown obtain.

Yearnings For Home

Oh let me go I'm weary here
And fevers scorch my brain,
I long to feel my native air
Breathe o'er each burning vein.

I long once more to see
My home among the distant hills,
To breathe amid the melody
Of murmering brooks and rills.

My home is where eternal snow
Round threat'ning craters sleep,
Where streamlets murmer soft and low
And playful cascades leap.

Tis where glad scenes shall meet
My weary, longing eye;
Where rocks and Alpine forests greet
The bright cerulean sky.

Your scenes are bright I know,
But there my mother pray'd,
Her cot is lowly, but I go
To die beneath its shade.

For, Oh I know she'll cling
'Round me her treasur'd long,
My sisters too will sing
Each lov'd familiar song.

They'll soothe my fever'd brow,
As in departed hours,
And spread around my dying couch
The brightest, fairest flowers.

FRANCES ELLEN WATKINS HARPER

Then let me go I'm weary here
And fevers scorch my brain,
I long to feel my native air,
Breathe o'er each burning vein.

Farewell, My Heart is Beating

Farewell, my heart is beating
With feelings sad and wild,
I've strove to hide its heaving
And 'mid my tears to smile.

This heart the lone and trusting,
Hath twin'd itself to thee;
And now when almost bursting,
Say, must it sever'd be.

When other brows for mine
Were alter'd, cold and strange,
I clasp'd my yearning heart to thine
And never found it chang'd.

This heart when almost breaking
Has leaned upon thy breast,
But when again 'tis aching
On thine it may not rest.

Oh clasp me closely ere we part
But breathe no sad farewell;
We can't be sever'd while thy heart
Retains o'er mine its spell.

HAMAN AND MORDECAI

He stood at Persia's Palace gate
And vassal round him bow'd,
Upon his brow was written hate
And he heeded not the crowd.

He heeded not the vassal throng
Whose praises rent the air,
His bosom shook with rage and scorn
For Mordecai stood there.

When ev'ry satrap bow'd
To him of noble blood,
Amid that servile crowd
One form unbending stood.

And as he gaz'd upon that form,
Dark flash'd his angry eye,
'Twas as the light'ning ere the storm
Hath swept in fury by.

On noble Mordecai alone,
He scorn'd to lay his hand;
But sought an edict from the throne
'Gainst all the captive band.

For full of pride and wrath
To his fell purpose true,
He vow'd that from his path
Should perish ev'ry Jew.

Then woman's voice arose
In deep impassion'd prayer,
Her fragile heart grew strong
'Twas the nervings of despair.

The king in mercy heard
Her pleading and her prayer
His heart with pity stirr'd,
And he resolved to spare.

And Haman met the fate
He'd for Mordecai decreed,
And from his cruel hate
The captive Jews are freed.

Let Me Love Thee

Let me love thee I have known
The agony deception brings,
And tho' my riven heart is lone
It fondly clasps and firmly clings.

Oh! let me love thee, I have seen
Hope's fairest blossoms fail,
Have felt my life a mournful dream
And this world a tearful vale.

Oh! let me love thee, I have felt
Deep yearnings for a kindly heart,
When joy would thrill or sorrow melt
Some kindred soul to bear a part.

Let me love thee, yet Oh! yet
Breathe not distrust around my heart,
The lov'd, the cherish may forget
And act a cold and faithless part.

Let me love thee, I have press'd
Sadly my aching heart and brow,
But banish'd ne'er from each recess
The thirst of love that fills them now.

Let me love thee, let my breast
Closely round thee entwine,
And hide within its deep recess
True constant love like thine.

Ruth and Naomi

Turn my daughters full of woe,
Is my heart so sad and lone,
Leave me, children, I would go
To my lov'd and distant home.

From my bosom death has torn,
Husband, children, all my stay;
Left me not a single one
For my life's declining day.

Want and wo surround my way,
Grief and famine where I tread;
In my native land they say
God is giving Jacob bread.

Naomi ceased, her daughters wept,
Their yearning hearts were fill'd,
Falling upon her wither'd neck
Their grief in tears distill'd.

Like rain upon a blighted tree
The tears of Orpah fell,
Kissing the pale and quiv'ring lip,
She breath'd her sad farewell.

But Ruth stood up, on her brow
There lay a heavenly calm,
And from her lips came soft and low
Words like a holy charm.

I will not leave thee, on thy brow
Are lines of sorrow, age and care,
Thy form is bent, thy step is slow,
Thy bosom stricken, lone and sear.

FRANCES ELLEN WATKINS HARPER

Thy failing lamp is growing dim,
It's flame is flick'ring past,
I will not leave thee withering,
'Neath stern affliction's blast.

When thy heart and home were glad,
I freely shar'd thy joyous lot
And now that heart is lone and sad,
Cease to entreat I'll leave thee not.

Oh if a lofty palace proud
Thy future home shall be,
Where sycophants around thee crowd
I'll share that home with thee.

And if on earth the humblest spot
Thy future home shall prove,
I'll bring into thy lowly cot
The wealth of woman's love.

However drear, earth has no lot
My spirit shrinks to share with thee,
Then mother, dear entreat me not
To turn from following after thee.

Go where thou wilt my steps are there,
Our path in life is one,
Thou hast no lot I will not share
Till life itself be done.

My country and home for thee
I freely, willingly resign;
Thy people shall my people be,
Thy God he shall be mine.

Then mother, dear, entreat me not
To turn from following thee,
My heart is mov'd to share thy lot
What e'er that lot may be.

"Bible Defence of Slavery"

Take sackcloth of the darkest dye
And shroud the pulpits round,
Servants of him that cannot lie
Sit mourning on the ground.

Let holy horror blanche each cheek,
Pale ev'ry brow with fears,
And rocks and stones if ye could speak
Ye well might melt to tears.

Let sorrow breathe in ev'ry tone
And grief in ev'ry strain ye raise,
Insult not heaven's majestic throne
With the mockery of praise.

A man whose light should be
The guide of age and youth,
Brings to the shrine of slavery
The sacrifice of truth.

For the fiercest wrongs that ever rose
Since Sodom's fearful cry,
The word of life has been unclos'd
To give your God the lie.

An infidel could do no more
To hide his country's guilty blot,
Than spread God's holy record o'er
The loathesome leprous spot.

Oh, when ye pray for heathen lands,
And plead for dark benighted shores,
Remember slavery's cruel hands
Make heathens at your doors.

To a Missionary

Joy, joy! unto the heathen,
Unfurl each snowy sail,
And waft the breath of prayer
On ev'ry breeze and gale.

Spread, spread your sails with mercy
As you plough the trackless,
And at your stern and helm
Shall God a vigil keep.

You're freighted with rich blessings,
You've glorious things to tell,
Your tidings are salvation,
Your theme Immanuel.

Heathen minds by sin degraded,
Captives 'neath the tempter's sway,
Shall from their moral vision
Have the darkness chas'd away.

'Neath bamboo hut and palm tree
Shall prayer like incense rise,
An oblation pure and holy
To the God of earth and skies.

He who from the fiery pillar
Guided once a pilgrim train,
Shall protect you by his power
As you sweep across the main.

More faithful than the needle
Pointing constant to the pole,
Shall the God of love be with you
When the darkest tempests roll.

God speed you on your journey,
May his presence and his power
Be your stay in grief and trial
And the joy of every hour.

"I Thirst"

I thirst, but earth cannot allay
The fever coursing thro' my veins,
The healing stream is far away,
It flows thro' Salem's glorious plains

The murmers of its crystal flow
Break ever o'er this world of strife,
My heart is weary let me go
To bathe it in the stream of life.

For a worn and weary heart
Hath bath'd in this pure stream,
And felt its griefs and cares depart
Like some forgotten dream.

THE DYING CHRISTIAN

The light was faintly streaming
Within a darken'd room,
Where a woman, faint and feeble
Was sinking to the tomb.

"The silver cord" was loosened,
We knew that she must die,
We read the mournful token
In the dimness of her eye.

We read it in the radiance
That lit her pallid cheek,
And the quivering of the feeble lip
Too faint its joys to speak.

We read in the glorious flash
Of strange unearthy light,
That ever and non would dash
The dimness from her sight.

And in the thoughts of living fire
Learn'd from God's encamping band,
Her words seem'd like a holy lyre
Tun'd in the spirit land.

Meet, oh meet me in the kingdom,
Said our lov'd and dying one,
I long to be with Jesus,
I am going, going home.

Like a child oppress'd with slumber
She calmly sank to rest,
With her trust in the Redeemer
And her head upon his breast.

She faded from our vision
Like a thing of love and light,
But we feel she lives forever
A spirit pure and bright.

A DREAM

I had a dream, a varied dream,
A dream of joy and dread;
Before me rose the judgement scene
For God had raised the dead.

Oh for an angel's hand to paint
The glories of that day,
When God did gather home each saint
And wipe their tears away.

Each waiting one lifted his head
Rejoic'd to see him nigh,
And earth cast out her sainted dead
To meet him in the sky.

Before his white and burning throne
A countless throng did stand;
Whilst Christ confess'd his own,
Whose names were on his hand.

I had a dream, a varied dream,
A dream of joy and dread;
Before me rose the judgment scene
For God had rais'd the dead.

Oh for an angel's hand to paint
The terrors of that day,
When God in vengeance for his saints
Girded himself with wrath to slay.

But, oh the terror, grief, and dread,
Tongue can't describe or pen portray;
When from their graves arose the dead,
Guilty to meet the judgment day.

As sudden as the lightning's flash
Across the sky doth sweep,
Earth's kingdom's were in pieces dash'd,
And waken'd from their guilty sleep.

I heard the agonizing cry,
Ye rocks and mountains on us fall,
And hide us from the Judge's eye,
But rocks and mounts fled from the call.

I saw the guilty ruin'd host
Standing before the burning throne,
The ruin'd, lost forever lost,
Whom God in wrath refus'd to own.

The Felon's Dream

He slept, but oh, it was not calm,
As in the days of infancy;
When sleep is nature's tender balm
To hearts from sorrow free.

He dream'd that fetters bound him fast,
He pin'd for liberty;
It seem'd deliverance came at last
And he from bonds were free.

In thought he journey'd where
Familiar voices rose,
Where not a brow was dim with care,
Or bosom heav'd with woes.

Around him press'd a happy band;
His wife and child drew near;
He felt the pressure of the hand,
And dried each falling tear.

His tender mother cast aside
The tears that dim'd her eye;
His father saw him as the pride
Of brighter days gone by.

He saw his wife around him cling,
He heard her breathe his name;
Oh! woman's love 's a precious thing,
A pure undying flame.

His brethren wept for manly pride,
May bend to woman's tears;
Then welcom'd round their fireside
The playmate of departed years.

His gentle sister fair and mild
Around him closely press'd,
She clasp'd his hand and smil'd
Then wept upon his breast.

All, all were glad around that hearth,
They hop'd his wanderings o'er;
That weary of the strange cold earth
He'd roam from them no more.

'Twas but a dream, 'twas fancy's flight
It mock'd his yearning heart;
It made his bosom feel its blight,
It probed him like a dart.

A prison held his fettered limbs,
Confinement was his lot,
No kindred voice rose to cheer,
He seem'd by friends and all forgot.

A Dialogue

Enquirer

Who hath a balm that will impart,
Strength to the fainting heart and brow;
I've look'd upon earth, and many a heart
Weary and wasting with woe.

Riches

I've heaps, I've heaps of shining dust,
I've gems from every mine;
Bid the weary spirit learn to trust
In gold that glitters, and gems that shine.

Enquirer

Oh! vain were the hopes of that heart,
Sighing its sorrows should cease,
That would search mid rubies and gems,
For the priceless pearl of peace.

Fame

I've wreaths, I've wreaths for the fever'd brow,
They're bright, and my name is fame;
Will not the heart forget its woe,
When I write it a deathless name?

Enquirer

No! your wreaths and laurels rare,
Would blanche and pale on a brow unblest;
While the heart, remindful of its care,
Would ache and throb with the same unrest.

FRANCES ELLEN WATKINS HARPER

Pleasure

Oh! I am queen of a laughing train,
The lightsome, the gay and glad;
I've a nectar cup for every pain,
They drink and forget to be sad.

Enquirer

But I have seen the cheek all pale,
When life was fading from the heart;
'Twas then I saw thy nectar fail,
I watch'd and saw thy smiles depart.

Religion

Oh! I am from the land of light,
My home is the world on high;
But I with the sons of night,
And bid their darkness fly.

I have no heaps of shining dust,
No gems from every mine;
But gifts to beautify the just,
On the brow of the pure to shine.

I have no wreaths of fading fame;
No records of decaying worth;
But God's remembrance and a name,
That can't be written in the earth.

When pleasure's smiles shall all depart,
Her nectar but increase the thirst,
I'll point the fever'd brow and heart,
To crystal founts that freshly burst.

Enquirer

Thy words do brighter hopes impart,
Than pleasure, wealth or fame;
Thou hast balm for the wounded heart,
Tell me, kind stranger, thy name.

My name and my nature is love;
God only wise, formed the plan
That mission'd me down from above,
As the guide and the solace of man.

Then I tell the fever'd brow and heart,
Thou'st balm for its wounds, and peace for its strife,
And the guerdon's which thou dost impart,
Are the pearl of peace and the crown of life.

FRANCES ELLEN WATKINS HARPER

CRUCIFIXION

The shadows of morning empurpled with light,
Bent o'er Judea, all lovely and bright;
The zephyr just risen, stole o'er the lea,
And dimpled the cheeks of river and sea.

On that bright morn, a clamor was heard,
The footsteps of men whose passions were stirred;
The voice of wrath, of tumult and strife,
'Twas the bloodthirsty cry of innocent life.

I gaz'd on their victim, on his pale brow,
'Mid beamings of love, were shadows of woe;
And his eyes, mid reproach and with'ring scorn,
Seemed like a star bending o'er a dark storm.

Tho' pale was his cheek, and ashy his brow,
By sorrow and anguish his spirit bent low;
Yet calm 'mid the fierce and cruel he stood,
Who, like beasts of the forests were eager for blood.

And this was the multitude fickle and vain,
Who hail'd him in triumph, as coming to reign;
Incited by priests, insatiate they stood,
Their cry was his life, their clamor his blood.

When dying earth drew round her form,
A mantle as dark as the vest of a storm,
Nature grew sad, earth trembled and shrank,
Astonish'd as Jesus the dire cup drank.

AN ACROSTIC

Angels bright that hover o'er thee,
Deem thee an object of their care;
Ever watchful they surround thee,
Lending aid when danger's near.

May this life, thus guarded, sister,
Always feel thy Saviour near;
Render him thy heart's devotion—
Trust his goodness, seek his care;
In these vales of grief and sorrow,
Nought shall harm while God is near.

For She Said If I May But Touch of His Clothes I Shall Be Whole

Life to her no brightness brought,
Pale and sorrow'd was her brow,
Till a bright and joyous thought,
Lit the darkness of her woe.

Long had sickness on her prayed;
Strength from every nerve had gone;
Skill and art could give no aid,
Thus her weary life passed on.

Like a sad and mornful dream,
Daily felt she life depart;
Hourly knew the vital stream,
Left the fountains of her heart.

He who'd lull'd the storm to rest,
Cleans'd the lepers, raised the dead;
Whilst a crowd around him prest
Near that suffering one did tread.

Nerv'd by blended hope and fear,
Reason'd thus her anxious heart,—
If to touch him I draw near,
All my suffering shall depart.

While the crowd around him stand,
I will touch, the sufferer said,—
Forth she reach'd her timid hand,
As she touch'd, her sickness fled.

"Who hath touch'd me." Jesus cried,
Virtue from my body's gone; From
the crowd a voice replied, Why
inquire, thousands throng.

Faint with fear thro' ev'ry limb,
Yet too grateful to deny;
Tremblingly, she knelt to him,
"Lord," she answered, "It was I."

Kindly, gently, Jesus said,
Words like balm unto her soul,
Peace upon her life be shed,
Child, thy faith has made thee whole.

The Presentiment

There's something strangely thrills my breast,
And fills it with a deep unrest,—
It is not grief, it is not pain,
Nor wish to live the past again.

'Tis something which I scarce can tell,
And yet I know, and feel it well;
Thro' ev'ry vein it seems to run,
And whispers life will soon be done.

It comes in accents soft and low,
Like bright streamlets crystal flow,
It whispers, lingers round my heart,
And tells me I must soon depart.

I felt it when the glow of life
Was warm upon my cheek,
In mornful cadence to my heart,
It solemnly did speak.

I felt it when a fearful strife
Was preying on my heart,
It told me from the cares of life,
I quickly must depart.

I felt it when my cheek grew pale,
By cares I could'nt repress;
It whisper'd to my wearried soul,
This earth is not your rest.

POEMS ON MISCELLANEOUS SUBJECTS

THE SYROPHENICIAN WOMAN

Joy to my bosom! rest to my fear!
Judea's prophet draweth near!
Joy to my bosom! peace to my heart!
Sickness and sorrow before him depart!

Rack'd with agony and pain,
Writhing long, my child has lain;
Now the prophet draweth near,
All our griefs shall disappear.

"Lord!" she cried, with mournful breath,
"Save! Oh, save my child from death!"
But as though she was unheard,
Jesus answered not a word.

With a purpose naught could move.
And the zeal of woman's love,
Down she knelt in anguish wild—
"Master! Save, Oh I save my child!"

"'Tis not meet," the Savior said,
"Thus, to waste the children's bread;
I am only sent to seek
Israel's lost and scattered sheep."

"True," she said, "Oh gracious Lord!
True and faithful is thy word;
But the humblest, meanest, may
Eat the crumbs they cast away."

"Woman," said the' astonish'd Lord,
"Be it even as thy word I
By thy faith that knows no fail,
Thou hast ask'd, and shalt prevail."

THE SLAVE MOTHER

Heard you that shriek? It rose
    So wildly on the air,
It seemed as if a burden'd heart
    Was breaking in despair.

Saw you those hands so sadly clasped—
    The bowed and feeble head—
The shuddering of that fragile form—
    That look of grief and dread?

Saw you the sad, imploring eye?
    Its every glance was pain,
As if a storm of agony
    Were sweeping through the brain.

She is a mother pale with fear,
    Her boy clings to her side,
And in her kirtle vainly tries
    His trembling form to hide.

He is not hers, although she bore
    For him a mother's pains;
He is not hers, although her blood
    Is coursing through his veins!

He is not hers, for cruel hands
    May rudely tear apart
The only wreath of household love
    That binds her breaking heart.

His love has been a joyous light
    That o'er her pathway smiled,
A fountain gushing ever new,
    Amid life's desert wild.

          FRANCES ELLEN WATKINS HARPER

His lightest word has been a tone
        Of music round her heart.
Their lives a streamlet blent in one—
        Oh, Father I must they part?

They tear him from her circling arms,
        Her last and fond embrace:—
Oh! never more may her sad eyes
        Gaze on his mournful face.

No marvel, then, these bitter shrieks
        Disturb the listening air;
She is a mother, and her heart
        Is breaking in despair.

Bible Defence of Slavery

Take sackcloth of the darkest dye,
And shroud the pulpits round!
Servants of him that cannot lie,
Sit mourning on the ground.

Let holy horror blanch each cheek,
Pale every brow with fears;
And rocks and stones, if ye could speak,
Ye well might melt to tears!

Let sorrow breathe in every tone,
In every strain ye raise;
Insult not God's majestic throne
With the' mockery of praise.

A "reverend" man, whose light should be
The guide of age and youth,
Brings to the shrine of Slavery
The sacrifice of truth!

For the direst wrong by man imposed,
Since Sodom's fearful cry.
The word of life has been unclos'd.
To give your God the lie.

Oh, I when ye pray for heathen lands.
And plead for their dark shores,
Remember Slavery's cruel hands
Make heathens at your doors!

Eliza Harris

Like a fawn from the arrow, startled and wild,
A woman swept by us, bearing a child;
In her eye was the night of a settled despair.
And her brow was o'ershaded with anguish and care.

She was nearing the river—in reaching the brink.
She heeded no danger, she paused not to think!
For she is a mother—her child is a slave—
And she'll give him his freedom or find him a grave!

T'was a vision to haunt us, that innocent face—
So pale in its aspect, so fair in its grace;
As the tramp of the horse and the hay of the hound,
With the fetters that gall, were trailing the ground!

She was nerv'd by despair, and strengthened by woe,
As she leap'd o'er the chasms that yawn'd from below;
Death howl'd in the tempest, and rav'd in the blast,
But she heard not the sound till the danger was past.

Oh! how shall I speak of my proud country's shame?
Of the stains on her glory, how give them their name?
How say that her banner in mockery waves—
Her "star-spangled banner"—o'er millions of slaves?

How say that the lawless may torture and chase
A woman whose crime is the hue of her face?
How the depths of the forest may echo around
With the shrieks of despair, and the bay of the hound?

With her step on the ice, and her arm on her child,
The danger was fearful, the pathway was wild;
But, aided by Heaven, she gained a free shore,
Where the friends of humanity open'd their door.

So fragile and lovely, so fearfully pale,
Like a lily that bends to the breath of the gale,
Save the heave of her breast, and the sway of her hair.
You'd have thought her a statue of fear and despair.

In agony close to her bosom she press'd
The life of her hearty the child of her breast:—
Oh! love from its tenderness gathering might,
Had strengthen'd er soul for the dangers of flight.

But she's free!—yes, free from the land where the slave
From the hand of oppression must rest in the grave;
Where bondage and torture, where scourges and chains,
Have plac'd on our banner indelible stains.

The bloodhounds have miss'd the scent of her way;
The hunter is rifled and foil'd of his prey;
Fierce jargon and cursing, with clanking of chains,
Make sounds of strange discord on Liberty's plains.

With the rapture of love and fullness of bliss,
She plac'd on his brow a mother's fond kiss:—
Oh! poverty, danger and death she can brave,
For the child of her love is no longer a slave!

FRANCES ELLEN WATKINS HARPER

ETHIOPIA

Yes! Ethiopia yet shall stretch
Her bleeding hands abroad;
Her cry of agony shall reach
The burning throne of God.

The tyrant's yoke from off her neck.
His fetters from her soul,
The mighty hand of God shall break,
And spurn the base control.

Redeemed from dust and freed from chains.
Her sons shall lift their eyes;
From cloud-capt hills and verdant plains
Shall shouts of triumph rise.

Upon her dark, despairing brow.
Shall play a smile of peace;
For God shall bend unto her wo,
And bid her sorrows cease.

'Neath sheltering vines and stately palms
Shall laughing children play,
And aged sires with joyous psalms
Shall gladden every day.

Secure by night, and blest by day,
Shall pass her hoppy hours;
Nor human tigers hunt for prey
Within her peaceful bowers.

Then, Ethiopia! stretch, oh! stretch
Thy bleeding hands abroad;
Thy cry of agony shall reach
And find redress from God.

THE DRUNKARD'S CHILD

He stood beside his dying child,
With a dim and bloodshot eye;
They'd won him from the haunts of vice
To see his first-born die.
He came with a slow and staggering tread,
A vague, unmeaning stare,
And, reeling, clasped the clammy hand,
So deathly pale and fair.

In a dark and gloomy chamber,
Life ebbing fast away.
On a coarse and wretched pallet,
The dying sufferer lay:
A smile of recognition
Lit up the glazing eye;
"I'm very glad," it seemed to say,
"You've come to see me die."

That smile reached to his callous heart,
Its sealed fountains stirred;
He tried to speak, but on his lips
Faltered and died each word.
And burning tears like rain
Poured down his bloated face.
Where guilt, remorse and shame
Had scathed, and left their trace.

"My father!" said the dying child,
(His Voice was faint and low,)
"Oh! clasp me closely to your heart.
And kiss me ere I go.
Bright angels beckon me away,
To the holy city fair—
Oh! tell me, father, ere I go,
Say, will you meet me there?"

FRANCES ELLEN WATKINS HARPER

He clasped him to his throbbing heart,
"I will! I will!" he said;
His pleading ceased—the father held
His first-born and his dead!
The marble brow, with golden curls.
Lay lifeless on his breast;
Like sunbeams on the distant clouds
Which line the gorgeous west.

The Slave Auction

The sale began—young girls were there,
Defenceless in their wretchedness,
Whose stifled sobs of deep despair
Revealed their anguish and distress.

And mothers stood, with streaming eyes,
And saw their dearest children sold;
Unheeded rose their bitter cries.
While tyrants bartered them for gold.

And woman, with her love and truth—
For these in sable forms may dwell—
Gaz'd on the husband of her youth,
With anguish none may paint or tell.

And men, whose sole crime was their hue,
The impress of their Maker's hand,
And frail and shrinking children, too,
Were gathered in that mournful band.

Ye who have laid your lov'd to rest.
And wept above their lifeless clay,
Know not the anguish of that breast.
Whose lov'd are rudely torn away.

Ye may not know how desolate
Are bosoms rudely forced to part.
And how a dull and heavy weight
Will press the life-drops from the heart.

FRANCES ELLEN WATKINS HARPER

The Revel

"He knoweth not that the dead are there."

In yonder halls reclining
Are forms surpassing fair,
And brilliant lights are shining,
But, oh! the dead are there!

There's music, song and dance,
There's banishment of care,
And mirth in every glance.
But, oh! the dead are there!

The wine cup's sparkling glow
Blends with the viands rare.
There is revelry and show.
But still, the dead are there!

'Neath that flow of song and mirth.
Runs the current of despair.
But the simple sons of earth
Know not the dead are there!

They'll shudder, start and tremble,
They'll weep in wild despair.
When the solemn truth breaks on them,
That the dead, the dead, are there!

THAT BLESSED HOPE

Oh! crush it not, that hope so blest,
Which cheers the fainting heart,
And points it to the coming rest.
Where sorrow has no part.

Tear from my heart each worldly prop.
Unbind each earthly string.
But to this blest and glorious hope,
Oh! let my spirit cling.

It cheered, amid the days of old.
Each holy patriarch's breast;
It was an anchor to their souls.
Upon it let me rest.

When wandering in dens and caves,
In sheep and goat skins dressed,
A peel'd and scattered people learned.
To know this hope was blest

Help me, amid this world of strife.
To long for Christ to reign,
That when He brings the crown of lift,
I may that crown obtain.

The Dying Christian

The light was faintly streaming
Within a darkened room,
Where a woman, faint and feeble.
Was sinking to the tomb.

The silver cord was loosened,
We knew that she must die;
We read the mournful token
In the dimness of her eye.

We read it in the radiance
That lit her pallid cheek,
And the quivering of the feeble lip,
Too faint its joys to speak.

Like a child oppressed with slumber,
She calmly sank to rest.
With her trust in the Redeemer,
And her head upon His breast.

She faded from our vision.
Like a thing of love and light;
But we feel she lives forever,
A spirit pure and bright.

Report

I Heard, my young friend,
You were seeking a wife,
A woman to make
Your companion for life.

Now, if you are seeking
A wife for your youth.
Let this be your aim, then—
Seek a woman of truth.

She may not have talents.
With greatness combined,
Her gifts may be humble,
Of person and mind:

But if she be constant.
And gentle, and true.
Believe me, my friend.
She's the woman for you!

Oh! wed not for beauty,
Though fair is the prize;
It may pall when you grasp it,
And fade in your eyes.

Let gold not allure you.
Let wealth not attract;
With a house full of treasure,
A woman may lack.

Let her habits be frugal,
Her hands not afraid
To work in her household,
Or follow her trade.

FRANCES ELLEN WATKINS HARPER

Let her language be modest.
Her actions discreet;
Her manners refined,
And free from deceit.

Now, if such you should find,
In your journey through life.
Just open your mind,
And make her your wife.

Advice to the Girls

Nay, do not blush! I only heard
You had a wish to marry;
I thought I'd speak a friendly word,
So just one moment tarry.

Wed not a man whose merit lies
In things of outward show,
In raven hair or flashing eyes,
That please your fancy so.

But marry tee who's good and kind,
And free from all pretence;
Who, if without a gifted mind.
At least has common sense.

SAVED BY FAITH

"She said, if I may but touch his clothes, I shall be whole."

Life to her no brightness brought.
Pale and stricken was her brow.
Till a bright and joyous thought
Lit the darkness of her woe.

Long had sickness on her preyed,
Strength from every nerve had gone;
Skill and art could give no aid:
Thus, her weary life passed on.

Like a sad and mournful dream,
Daily felt she life depart.
Hourly knew the vital stream
Left the fountain of her heart.

He who lull'd the storm to rest,
Cleans'd the lepers, rais'd the dead,
Whilst a crowd around him pressed,
Near that suffering one did tread.

Nerv'd by blended hope and fear,
Reasoned thus her anxious heart:
"If to touch him I draw near,
All my suffering shall depart.

While the crowd around him stand,
I will touch," the sufferer said;
Forth she reached her timid hand—
As she touched, her sickness fled.

"Who hath touched me?" Jesus cried;
"Virtue from my body's gone."
From the crowd a voice replied,
"Why inquire in such a throng?"

Faint with fear through every limb,
Yet too grateful to deny.
Tremblingly she knelt to him,
"Lord!" she answered, "it was I!"

Kindly, gently, Jesus said—
Words like balm unto her soul—
"Peace upon thy life be shed!
Child! thy faith hath made thee whole!"

DIED OF STARVATION

They forced him into prison,
  Because he begged for bread;
"My wife is starving—dying!"
  In vain the poor man plead.[1]

They forced him into prison,
  Strong bars enclosed the walls,
While the rich and proud were feasting
  Within their sumptuous halls.

He'd striven long with anguish.
  Had wrestled with despair;
But his weary heart was breaking
  'Neath its crushing load of care.

And he prayed them in that prison,
  "Oh, let me seek my wife!"
For he knew that want was feeding,
  On the remnant of her life.

That night his wife lay moaning
  Upon her bed in pain;
Hunger gnawing at her vitals,
  Fever scorching through her brain.

She wondered at his tarrying,
  He was not wont to stay;
Mid hunger, pain and watching.
  The moments waned away.

Sadly crouching by the embers,
  Her famished children lay;
And she longed to gaze upon them.
  As her spirit passed away.

---

1. See this case, as touchingly related, in *Oliver Twist* by Dickens.

But the embers were too feeble,
She could not see each face.
So she clasped her arms around them—
'Twas their mother's last embrace.

They loosed him from his prison.
As a felon from his chain;
Though his strength was hunger bitter,
He sought his home again.

Just as her spirit lingered
On Time's receding shore.
She heard his welcome footstep
On the threshold of the door.

He was faint and spirit-broken.
But, rousing from despair,
He clasped her icy fingers,
As she breathed her dying prayer.

With a gentle smile and blessing,
Her spirit winged its flight,
As the room, in all its glory.
Bathed the world in dazzling light.

There was weeping, bitter weeping.
In the chamber of the dead.
For well the stricken husband knew
She had died for want of bread.

A Mother's Heroism

"When the noble mother of LOVEJOY heard of her son's death, she said, 'It is well! I had rather he should die so than desert his principles.'"

The murmurs of a distant strife
Fell on a mother's ear;
Her son had yielded up his life,
Mid scenes of wrath and fear.

They told her how he'd spent his breath
In pleading for the dumb,
And how the glorious martyr wreath
Her child had nobly won.

They told her of his courage high.
Mid brutal force and might;
How he had nerved himself to die,
In battling for the right.

It seemed as if a fearful storm
Swept wildly round her soul;
A moment, and her fragile form
Bent 'neath its fierce control.

From lip and brow the color fled—
But light flashed to her eye:
"'T is well! 't is well!" the mother said,
"That thus my child should die."

"'T is well that, to his latest breath,
He plead for liberty;
Truth nerved him for the hour of death,
And taught him how to die."

"It taught him how to cast aside
Earth's honors and renown;
To trample on her fame and pride.
And win a martyr's crown."

The Fugitive's Wife

It was my sad and weary lot
To toil in slavery;
But one thing cheered my lowly cot-
My husband was with me.

One evening, as our children played
Around our cabin door,
I noticed on his brow a shade
I'd never seen before;

And in his eyes a gloomy night
Of anguish and despair;—
I gazed upon their troubled light,
To read the meaning there.

He strained me to his heaving heart—
My own beat wild with fear;
I knew not, but I sadly felt
There must be evil near.

He vainly strove to cast aside
The tears that fell like rain:—
Too frail, indeed, is manly pride,
To strive with grief and pain.

Again he clasped me to his breast,
And said that we must part:
I tried to speak—but, oh! it seemed
An arrow reached my heart.

"Bear not," I cried, "unto your grave.
The yoke you've borne from birth;
No longer live a helpless slave.
The meanest thing on earth!"

FRANCES ELLEN WATKINS HARPER

The Contrast

They scorned her for her sinning.
Spoke harshly of her fall.
Nor lent the hand of mercy
To break her hated thrall.

The dews of meek repentance
Stood in her downcast eye:
Would no one heed her anguish?
All pass her coldly by?

From the cold, averted glances
Of each reproachful eye,
She turned aside, heart-broken,
And laid her down to die.

And where was he, who sullied
Her once unspotted name;
Who lured her from life's brightness
To agony and shame?

Who left her on Life's billows,
A wrecked and ruined thing;
Who brought the winter of despair
Upon Hope's blooming spring?

Through the halls of wealth and fashion.
In gaiety and pride.
He was leading to the altar
A fair and lovely bride!

None scorned him for his sinning,
Few saw it through his gold;
His crimes were only foibles.
And these were gently told.

Before him rose a vision,
A maid of beauty rare;
Then a pale, heart-broken woman,
The image of despair.

Next came a sad procession,
With many a sob and tear;
A widow'd, childless mother
Totter'd by an humble bier.

The vision quickly faded,
The sad, unwelcome sight;
But his lip forgot its laughter,
And his eye its careless light

A moment, and the flood-gates
Of memory opened wide;
And remorseful recollection
Flowed like a lava tide.

That widow's wail of anguish
Seemed strangely blending there,
And mid the soft lights floated
That image of despair.

The Prodigal's Return

He came—a wanderer—years of sin
Had blanched his blooming cheek,
Telling a tale of strife within.
That words might vainly speak.

His feet were bare, his garments torn,
His brow was deadly white;
His heart was bleeding, crushed and worn.
His soul had felt a blight.

His father saw him; pity swept
And yearn'd through every vein;
He ran and clasp'd his child, and wept,
Murm'ring, "He lives again!"

"Father, I've come, but not to claim
Aught from thy love or grace;
I come, a child of guilt and shame.
To beg a servant's place."

"Enough! Enough!" the father said,
"Bring robes of princely cost!"—
The past with all its shadows fled,
For now was found the lost.

"Put shoes upon my poor child's feet.
With rings his hand adorn,
And bid my house his coming greet
With music, dance and song."

Oh, Savior! mid this world of strife.
When wayward here we roam.
Conduct us to the paths of life,
And guide us safely home.

Then in thy holy courts above,
Thy praise our lips shall sound,
While angels join our song of love,
That we, the lost, are found!

Eva's Farewell

Farewell, father! I am dying,
Going to the "glory land,"
Where the sun is ever shining.
And the zephyr's ever bland;

Where the living fountains flowing.
Quench the pining spirit's thirst;
Where the tree of life is growing.
Where the crystal fountains burst.

Father! hear that music holy
Floating from the spirit land!
At the pearly gates of glory.
Radiant angels waiting stand.

Father! kiss your dearest Eva,
Press her cold and clammy hand.
Ere the glittering hosts receive her,
Welcome to their cherub band.

MISCELLANEOUS WRITINGS

CHRISTIANITY

Christianity is a system claiming God for its author, and the welfare of man for its object. It is a system so uniform, exalted, and pure, that the loftiest intellects have acknowledged its influence, and acquiesced in the justness of its claims. Genius has bent from his erratic course to gather fire from her altars, and pathos from the agony of Gethsemane and the sufferings of Calvary. Philosophy and science have paused amid their speculative researches and wondrous revelations, to gain wisdom from her teachings and knowledge from her precepts. Poetry has culled her fairest flowers and wreathed her softest, to bind her Author's "bleeding brow." Music has strung her sweetest lyres and breathed her noblest strains to celebrate his fame; whilst Learning has brought her richest pearls and rarest gems to lay at her feet and has bent from her lofty heights to bow at the lowly cross. The constant friend of man, she has stood by him in his hour of greatest need. She has cheered the prisoner in his cell and strengthened the martyr at the stake. She has nerved the frail and shrinking heart of woman for high and holy deeds. The worn and weary have rested their fainting heads upon her bosom, and gathered strength from her words and courage from her counsels. She has been the staff of decrepit age, and the joy of manhood in its strength. She has bent over the form of lovely childhood and suffered it to have a place in the Redeemer's arms. She has stood by the bed of the dying and unveiled the glories of eternal life; gilding the darkness of the tomb with the glory of the resurrection.

Christianity has changed the moral aspect of nations. Idolatrous temples have crumbled at her touch, and Guilt 'owned its deformity in her presence. The darkest habitations of earth have been irradiated with heavenly light, and the death-shriek of immolated victims changed for ascriptions of praise to God and the Lamb. Envy and Malice have been rebuked by her contented look, and fretful Impatience by her gentle and resigned manner.

At her approach, fetters have been broken, and men have risen redeemed from dust, and freed from chains. Manhood has learned its dignity and worth; its kindred with angels, and alliance to God.

To man, guilty, fallen, and degraded man, she shows a fountain drawn from the Redeemer's veins; there she bids him wash and be clean. She points him to "Mount Zion, to the city of the living God, to an innumerable company of angels, to the spirits of just men made perfect, and to Jesus, the Mediator of the New Covenant," and urges him to rise from the degradation of sin, renew his nature, and join with them. She shows a pattern so spotless and holy, so elevated and pure, that he might shrink from it discouraged, did she not bring with her a promise from the lips of Jehovah, that he would give power to the faint and might to those who have no strength. Learning may bring her ample pages, and her ponderous records, rich with the spoils of every age, gathered from every land, and gleaned from every source. Philosophy and science may bring their abstruse researches and wondrous revelations—Literature her elegance, with the toils of the pen and the labors of the pencil—but they are idle tales, compared to the truths of Christianity. They may cultivate the intellect, enlighten the understanding, give scope to the imagination, and refine the sensibilities; but they open not, to our dim eyes and longing vision, the land of crystal founts and deathless flowers. Philosophy searches earth; Religion opens heaven. Philosophy doubts and tremble at the portals of eternity; Religion lifts the veil, and shows us golden streets, lit by the Redeemer's countenance, and irradiated by his smile. Philosophy strives to reconcile us to death; Religion triumphs over it.

Philosophy treads amid the pathway of stars and stands a delighted listener to the music of the spheres; but Religion gazes on the glorious palaces of. God, while the harpings of the bloodwashed, and the songs of the redeemed, fall upon her ravished ear. Philosophy has her place; Religion her important sphere; one is of importance here, the other of infinite and vital importance, both here and hereafter.

THE BIBLE

Amid ancient lore and modern learning, the Word of God stands unique and preeminent. Wonderful in its construction, admirable in its adaptation, it contains truths that a child may comprehend, and mysteries into which angels desire to look. It is in harmony with that adaptation of ends to means which pervades creation, from the polypus tribes, elaborating their coral homes, to man, the wondrous work of God. It forms the brightest link of that glorious chain which unites the humblest work of creation with the throne of the infinite and eternal Jehovah. As light, with its infinite particles and curiously blended colors, is suited to an eye prepared for the alternations of day; as air, with its subtle and invisible essence, is fitted for the delicate organs of respiration; and, in a word, as this material world is adapted to man's physical nature, so the word of eternal truth is adapted to his moral nature and mental constitution. It finds him wounded, sick and suffering, and points him to the balm of Gilead and the Physician of souls. It finds him stained by transgression and defiled with guilt, and directs him to the "blood that cleanseth from all unrighteousness and sin." It finds him athirst and faint, pining amid the deserts of life, and shows him the wells of salvation and the rivers of life. It addresses itself to his moral and spiritual nature, makes provision for his wants and weaknesses, and meets his yearnings and aspirations. It is adapted to his mind in its earliest stages of progression, and its highest state of intellectuality. It provides light for his darkness, joy for his anguish, a solace for his woes, balm for his wounds, and heaven for his hopes. It unveils the unseen world and reveals. Him who is the light of creation and the joy of the universe, reconciled through the death of His Son. It promises the faithful a blessed reunion, in a land undimmed with tears, undarkened by sorrow. It affords a truth for the living, and a refuge for the dying. Aided by the Holy Spirit, it guides us through life, points out the shoals, the quicksands and hidden rocks which endanger our path, and at last leaves us with the eternal God for our refuge, and his everlasting arms for our protection.

The Colored People in America

Having been placed by a dominant race in circumstances over which we have had no control, we have been the butt of ridicule and the mark of oppression. Identified with a people over whom weary ages of degradation have passed, whatever concerns them, as a race, concerns me. I have noticed among our people a disposition to censure and upbraid each other,—a disposition which has its foundation rather, perhaps, in a want of common sympathy and consideration, than mutual hatred or other unholy passions. Born to an inheritance of misery, nurtured in degradation, and cradled in oppression, with the scorn of the white man upon their souls, his fetters upon their limbs, his scourge upon their flesh, what can be expected from their offspring, but a mournful reaction of that cursed system which spreads its baneful influence over body and soul; which dwarfs the intellect, stunts its development, debases the spirit, and degrades the soul? Place any nation in the same condition which has been our hapless lot, fetter their limbs and degrade their souls, debase their sons and corrupt their daughters; and, when the restless yearnings for liberty shall burn through heart and brain—when, tortured by wrong and goaded by oppression, the hearts that would madden with misery, or break in despair, resolve to break their thrall and escape from bondage, then let the bay of the bloodhound and the scent of the human tiger be upon their track;—let them feel that, from the ceaseless murmur of the Atlantic to the sullen roar of the Pacific, from the thunders of the rainbow-crowned Niagara to the swollen waters of the Mexican gulf, they have no shelter for their bleeding feet, or resting place for their defenceless heads;—let them, when nominally free, feel that they have only exchanged the iron yoke of oppression for the galling fetters of a vitiated public opinion;—let prejudice assign them the lowest places and the humblest positions, and make them "hewers of wood and drawers of water;"—let their income be so small that they must from necessity bequeath to their children an inheritance of poverty and a limited education,—and tell me, reviler of our race! censurer of our people! if there is a nation in whose veins runs the purest Caucasian blood, upon whom the same causes would not produce the same effects; whose social condition, intellectual and moral character, would present a more favorable aspect than ours?

FRANCES ELLEN WATKINS HARPER

But there is hope; yes, "blessed be God!" for our downtrodden and despised race. Public and private schools accommodate our children; and in my own Southern home, I see women whose lot is unremitted labor, saving a pittance from their scanty wages to defray the expense of learning to read. We have papers edited by colored editors, which we may consider an honor to possess and a credit to sustain. We have a church that is extending itself from east to west, from north to south, through poverty and reproach, persecution, and pain. We have our faults, our want of union and concentration of purpose; but are there not extenuating circumstances around our darkest faults—palliating excuses for our most egregious errors? and shall we not hope, that the mental and moral aspect which we present is but the first step of a mighty advancement, the faintest coruscations of the day that will dawn with unclouded splendor upon our down-trodden and benighted race, and that ere long we may present to the admiring gaze of those who wish us well, a people to whom knowledge has given power, and righteousness exaltation?

Free Labor

I wear an easy garment,
    O'er it no toiling slave
Wept tears of hopeless anguish,
    In his passage to the grave.
And from its ample folds
    Shall rise no cry to God,
Upon its warp and woof shall be
    No stain of tears and blood.
Oh, lightly shall it press my form,
    Unladened with a sigh,
I shall not 'mid its rustling hear,
    Some sad despairing cry.
This fabric is too light to bear
    The weight of bondsmen's tears,
I shall not in its texture trace
    The agony of years.
Too light to bear a smother'd sigh,
    From some lorn woman's heart,
Whose only wreath of household love
    Is rudely torn apart.
Then lightly shall it press my form,
    Unburden'd by a sigh;
And from its seams and folds shall rise,
    No voice to pierce the sky,
And witness at the throne of God,
    In language deep and strong,
That I have nerv'd Oppression's hand,
    For deeds of guilt and wrong.

Bury Me in a Free Land

Make me a grave where'er you will,
In a lowly plain, or a lofty hill;
Make it among earth's humblest graves,
But not in a land where men are slaves.

I could not rest if around my grave
I heard the steps of a trembling slave;
His shadow above my silent tomb
Would make it a place of fearful gloom.

I could not rest if I heard the tread
Of a coffle gang to the shambles led,
And the mother's shriek of wild despair
Rise like a curse on the trembling air.

I could not sleep if I saw the lash
Drinking her blood at each fearful gash,
And I saw her babes torn from her breast,
Like trembling doves from their parent nest.

I'd shudder and start if I heard the bay
Of bloodhounds seizing their human prey,
And I heard the captive plead in vain
As they bound afresh his galling chain.

If I saw young girls from their mother's arms
Bartered and sold for their youthful charms,
My eye would flash with a mournful flame,
My death-paled cheek grow red with shame.

I would sleep, dear friends, where bloated might
Can rob no man of his dearest right;
My rest shall be calm in any grave
Where none can call his brother a slave.

I ask no monument, proud and high,
To arrest the gaze of the passers-by;
All that my yearning spirit craves,
Is bury me not in a land of slaves.

Two Offers

W hat is the matter with you, Laura, this morning? I have been watching you this hour, and in that time you have commenced a half dozen letters and torn them all up. What matter of such grave moment is puzzling your dear little head, that you do not know how to decide?"

"Well, it is an important matter: I have two offers for marriage, and I do not know which to choose."

"I should accept neither, or to say the least, not at present."

"Why not?"

"Because I think a woman who is undecided between two offers, has not love enough for either to make a choice; and in that very hesitation, indecision, she has a reason to pause and seriously reflect, lest her marriage, instead of being an affinity of souls or a union of hearts, should only be a mere matter of bargain and sale, or an affair of convenience and selfish interest."

"But I consider them both very good offers, just such as many a girl would gladly receive. But to tell you the truth, I do not think that I regard either as a woman should the man she chooses for her husband. But then if I refuse, there is the risk of being an old maid, and that is not to be thought of."

"Well, suppose there is, is that the most dreadful fate that can befall a woman? Is there not more intense wretchedness in an ill-assorted marriage—more utter loneliness in a loveless home, than in the lot of the old maid who accepts her earthly mission as a gift from God, and strives to walk the path of life with earnest and unfaltering steps?"

"Oh! what a little preacher you are. I really believe that you were cut out for an old maid; that when nature formed you, she put in a double portion of intellect to make up for a deficiency of love; and yet you are kind and affectionate. But I do not think that you know anything of the grand, over-mastering passion, or the deep necessity of woman's heart for loving."

"Do you think so?" resumed the first speaker; and bending over her work she quietly applied herself to the knitting that had lain neglected by her side, during this brief conversation; but as she did so, a shadow flitted over her pale and intellectual brow, a mist gathered in her eyes, and a slight quivering of the lips, revealed a depth of feeling to which her companion was a stranger.

But before I proceed with my story, let me give you a slight history of the speakers. They were cousins, who had met life under different auspices. Laura Lagrange, was the only daughter of rich and indulgent parents, who had spared no pains to make her an accomplished lady.

Her cousin, Janette Alston, was the child of parents, rich only in goodness and affection. Her father had been unfortunate in business, and dying before he could retrieve his fortunes, left his business in an embarrassed state.

His widow was unacquainted with his business affairs, and when the estate was settled, hungry creditors had brought their claims and the lawyers had received their fees, she found herself homeless and almost penniless, and she who had been sheltered in the warm clasp of loving arms, found them too powerless to shield her from the pitiless pelting storms of adversity.

Year after year she struggled with poverty and wrestled with want, till her toil-worn hands became too feeble to hold the shattered chords of existence, and her tear-dimmed eyes grew heavy with the slumber of death.

Her daughter had watched over her with untiring devotion, had closed her eyes in death, and gone out into the busy, restless world, missing a precious tone from the voices of earth, a beloved step from the paths of life.

Too self reliant to depend on the charity of relations, she endeavored to support herself by her own exertions, and she had succeeded. Her path for a while was marked with struggle and trial, but instead of uselessly repining, she met them bravely, and her life became not a thing of ease and indulgence, but of conquest, victory, and accomplishments.

At the time when this conversation took place, the deep trials of her life had passed away. The achievements of her genius had won her a position in the literary world, where she shone as one of its bright particular stars. And with her fame came a competence of worldly means, which gave her leisure for improvement, and the riper development of her rare talents.

And she, that pale intellectual woman, whose genius gave life and vivacity to the social circle, and whose presence threw a halo of beauty and grace around the charmed atmosphere in which she moved, had at one period of her life, known the mystic and solemn strength of an all-absorbing love. Years faded into the misty past, had seen the kindling of her eye, the quick flushing of her cheek, and the wild throbbing of her heart, at tones of a voice long since hushed to the stillness of death.

Deeply, wildly, passionately, she had loved. Her whole life seemed like the pouring out of rich, warm and gushing affections. This love quickened her talents, inspired her genius, and threw over her life a tender and spiritual earnestness. And then came a fearful shock, a mournful waking from that "dream of beauty and delight."

A shadow fell around her path; it came between her and the object of her heart's worship; first a few cold words, estrangement, and then a painful separation; the old story of woman's pride—digging the sepulchre of her happiness, and then a new-made grave, and her path over it to the spirit world; and thus faded out from that young heart her bright, brief and saddened dream of life.

Faint and spirit-broken, she turned from the scenes associated with the memory of the loved and lost. She tried to break the chain of sad associations that bound her to the mournful past; and so, pressing back the bitter sobs from her almost breaking heart, like the dying dolphin, whose beauty is born of its death anguish, her genius gathered strength from suffering and wondrous power and brilliancy from the agony she hid within the desolate chambers of her soul.

Men hailed her as one of earth's strangely gifted children, and wreathed the garlands of fame for her brow, when it was throbbing with a wild and fearful unrest. They breathed her name with applause, when through the lonely halls of her stricken spirit, was an earnest cry for peace, a deep yearning for sympathy and heart-support.

But life, with its stern realities, met her; its solemn responsibilities confronted her, and turning, with an earnest and shattered spirit, to life's duties and trials, she found a calmness and strength that she had only imagined in her dreams of poetry and song.

We will now pass over a period of ten years, and the cousins have met again. In that calm and lovely woman, in whose eyes is a depth of tenderness, tempering the flashes of her genius, whose looks and tones are full of sympathy and love, we recognize the once smitten and stricken Janette Alston.

The bloom of her girlhood had given way to a higher type of spiritual beauty, as if some unseen hand had been polishing and refining the temple in which her lovely spirit found its habitation; and this had been the fact. Her inner life had grown beautiful, and it was this that was constantly developing the outer.

Never, in the early flush of womanhood, when an absorbing love had lit up her eyes and glowed in her life, had she appeared so interesting as when, with a countenance which seemed overshadowed with a spiritual light, she bent over the death-bed of a young woman, just lingering at the shadowy gates of the unseen land.

"Has he come?" faintly but eagerly exclaimed the dying woman. "Oh! how I have longed for his coming, and even in death he forgets me."

"Oh, do not say so, dear Laura, some accident may have detained him," said Janette to her cousin; for on that bed, from whence she will never rise, lies the once-beautiful and lighthearted Laura Lagrange, the brightness of whose eyes has long since been dimmed with tears, and whose voice had become like a harp whose every chord is turned to sadness—whose faintest thrill and loudest vibrations are but the variations of agony.

A heavy hand was laid upon her once warm and bounding heart, and a voice came whispering through her soul, that she must die. But, to her, the tidings was a message of deliverance—a voice, hushing her wild sorrows to the calmness of resignation and hope. Life had grown so weary upon her head—the future looked so hopeless—she had no wish to tread again the track where thorns had pierced her feet, and clouds overcast her sky; and she hailed the coming of death's angel as the footsteps of a welcome friend.

And yet, earth had one object so very dear to her weary heart. It was her absent and recreant husband; for, since that conversation, she had accepted one of her offers, and become a wife. But, before she married, she learned that great lesson of human experience and woman's life, to love the man who bowed at her shrine, a willing worshipper.

He had a pleasing address, raven hair, flashing eyes, a voice of thrilling sweetness, and lips of persuasive eloquence; and being well versed in the ways of the world, he won his way to her heart, and she became his bride, and he was proud of his prize.

Vain and superficial in his character, he looked upon marriage not as a divine sacrament for the soul's development and human progression, but as the title-deed that gave him possession of the woman he thought he loved.

But alas for her, the laxity of his principles had rendered him unworthy of the deep and undying devotion of a pure-hearted woman; but, for awhile, he hid from her his true character, and she blindly loved him, and for a short period was happy in the consciousness of being beloved; though sometimes a vague unrest would fill her soul, when, overflowing with a sense of the good, the beautiful, and the true, she would turn to him, but find no response to the deep yearnings of her soul—no appreciation of life's highest realities—its solemn grandeur and significant importance.

Their souls never met, and soon she found a void in her bosom, that his earth-born love could not fill. He did not satisfy the wants of her mental and moral nature—between him and her there was no affinity of minds, no intercommunion of souls.

Talk as you will of woman's deep capacity for loving, of the strength of her affectional nature. I do not deny it; but will the mere possession of any human love, fully satisfy all the demands of her whole being? You may paint her in poetry or fiction, as a frail vine, clinging to her brother man for support, and dying when deprived of it; and all this may sound well enough to please the imaginations of school-girls, or love-lorn maidens.

But woman—the true woman—if you would render her happy, it needs more than the mere development of her affectional nature. Her conscience should be enlightened, her faith in the true and right established, scope given to her Heaven-endowed and God-given faculties.

The true aim of female education should be not a development of one or two, but all the faculties of the human soul, because no perfect womanhood is developed by imperfect culture. Intense love is often akin to intense suffering, and to trust the whole wealth of a woman's nature on the frail bark of human love, may often be like trusting a cargo of gold and precious gems, to a bark that has never battled with the storm, or buffeted the waves.

Is it any wonder, then, that so many life-barks go down, paving the ocean of time with precious hearts and wasted hopes? that so many float around us, shattered and dismasted wrecks? that so many are stranded on the shoals of existence, mournful beacons and solemn warnings for the thoughtless, to whom marriage is a careless and hasty rushing together of the affections?

Alas that an institution so fraught with good for humanity should be so perverted, and that state of life, which should be filled with happiness, become so replete with misery.

And this was the fate of Laura Lagrange. For a brief period after her marriage her life seemed like a bright and beautiful dream, full of hope and radiant with joy. And then there came a change—he found other attractions that lay beyond the pale of home influences.

The gambling saloon had power to win him from her side, he had lived in an element of unhealthy and unhallowed excitements, and the society of a loving wife, the pleasures of a well-regulated home, were enjoyments too tame for one who had vitiated his tastes by the pleasures of sin.

There were charmed houses of vice, built upon dead men's loves, where, amid the flow of song, laughter, wine, and careless mirth, he would spend hour after hour, forgetting the cheek that was paling through his neglect, heedless of the tear-dimmed eyes, peering anxiously into the darkness, waiting, or watching his return.

The influence of old associations was upon him. In early life, home had been to him a place of ceilings and walls, not a true home, built upon goodness, love and truth. It was a place where velvet carpets hushed its tread, where images of loveliness and beauty invoked into being by painter's art and sculptor's skill, pleased the eye and gratified the taste, where magnificence surrounded his way and costly clothing adorned his person; but it was not the place for the true culture and right development of his soul.

His father had been too much engrossed in making money, and his mother in spending it, in striving to maintain a fashionable position in society, and shining in the eyes of the world, to give the proper direction to the character of their wayward and impulsive son. His mother put beautiful robes upon his body, but left ugly scars upon his soul; she pampered his appetite, but starved his spirit.

Every mother should be a true artist, who knows how to weave into her child's life images of grace and beauty, the true poet capable of writing on the soul of childhood the harmony of love and truth, and teaching it how to produce the grandest of all poems—the poetry of a true and noble life.

But in his home, a love for the good, the true and right, had been sacrificed at the shrine of frivolity and fashion. That parental authority which should have been preserved as a string of precious pearls, unbroken and unscattered, was simply the administration of chance.

At one time obedience was enforced by authority, at another time by flattery and promises, and just as often it was not enforced at all. His early associations were formed as chance directed, and from his want of home-training, his character received a bias, his life a shade, which ran through every avenue of his existence, and darkened all his future hours.

Oh, if we would trace the history of all the crimes that have o'ershadowed this sin-shrouded and sorrow-darkened world of ours, how many might be seen arising from the wrong home influences, or the weakening of the home ties.

Home should always be the best school for the affections, the birthplace of high resolves, and the altar upon which lofty aspirations are kindled, from whence the soul may go forth strengthened, to act its part aright in the great drama of life with conscience enlightened, affections cultivated, and reason and judgment dominant.

But alas for the young wife. Her husband had not been blessed with such a home. When he entered the arena of life, the voices from home did not linger around his path as angels of guidance about his steps; they were not like so many messages to invite him to deeds of high and holy worth.

The memory of no sainted mother arose between him and deeds of darkness; the earnest prayers of no father arrested him in his downward course: and before a year of his married life had waned, his young wife had learned to wait and mourn his frequent and uncalled-for absence.

More than once had she seen him come home from his midnight haunts, the bright intelligence of his eye displaced by the drunkard's stare, and his manly gait changed to the inebriate's stagger; and she was beginning to know the bitter agony that is compressed in the mournful words, a drunkard's wife.

And then there came a bright but brief episode in her experience; the angel of life gave to her existence a deeper meaning and loftier significance; she sheltered in the warm clasp of her loving arms, a dear babe, a precious child, whose love filled every chamber of her heart, and felt the fount of maternal love gushing so new within her soul. That child was hers.

How overshadowing was the love with which she bent over its helplessness, how much it helped to fill the void and chasms in her soul. How many lonely hours were beguiled by its winsome ways, its answering smiles and fond caresses. How exquisite and solemn was the feeling that thrilled her heart when she clasped the tiny hands together and taught her dear child to call God "Our Father."

What a blessing was that child. The father paused in his headlong career, awed by the strange beauty and precocious intellect of his child;

and the mother's life had a better expression through her ministrations of love. And then there came hours of bitter anguish, shading the sunlight of her home and hushing the music of her heart.

The angel of death bent over the couch of her child and beaconed it away. Closer and closer the mother strained her child to her wildly heaving breast, and struggled with the heavy hand that lay upon its heart. Love and agony contended with death, and the language of the mother's heart was,

> *"Oh, Death, away! that innocent is mine;*
> *I cannot spare him from my arms*
> *To lay him, Death, in thine.*
> *I am a mother, Death; I gave that darling birth*
> *I could not bear his lifeless limbs*
> *Should moulder in the earth."*

But death was stronger than love and mightier than agony and won the child for the land of crystal founts and deathless flowers, and the poor, stricken mother sat down beneath the shadow of her mighty grief, feeling as if a great light had gone out from her soul, and that the sunshine had suddenly faded around her path. She turned in her deep anguish to the father of her child, the loved and cherished dead.

For awhile his words were kind and tender, his heart seemed subdued, and his tenderness fell upon her worn and weary heart like rain on perishing flowers, or cooling waters to lips all parched with thirst and scorched with fever; but the change was evanescent, the influence of unhallowed associations and evil habits had vitiated and poisoned the springs of his existence.

They had bound him in their meshes, and he lacked the moral strength to break his fetters, and stand erect in all the strength and dignity of a true manhood, making life's highest excellence his ideal, and striving to gain it.

And yet moments of deep contrition would sweep over him, when he would resolve to abandon the wine-cup forever, when he was ready to forswear the handling of another card, and he would try to break away from the associations that he felt were working his ruin; but when the hour of temptation came his strength was weakness, his earnest purposes were cobwebs, his well meant resolutions ropes of sand, and thus passed year after year of the married life of Laura Lagrange.

FRANCES ELLEN WATKINS HARPER

She tried to hide her agony from the public gaze, to smile when her heart was almost breaking. But year after year her voice grew fainter and sadder, her once light and bounding step grew slower and faltering. Year after year she wrestled with agony, and strove with despair, till the quick eyes of her brother read, in the paling of her cheek and the dimming eye, the secret anguish of her worn and weary spirit. On that wan, sad face, he saw the death-tokens, and he knew the dark wing of the mystic angel swept coldly around her path.

"Laura," said her brother to her one day, "you are not well, and I think you need our mother's tender care and nursing. You are daily losing strength, and if you will go I will accompany you." At first, she hesitated, she shrank almost instinctively from presenting that pale sad face to the loved ones at home. That face was such a telltale; it told of heart-sickness, of hope deferred, and the mournful story of unrequited love.

But then a deep yearning for home sympathy woke within her a passionate longing for love's kind words, for tenderness and heart support, and she resolved to seek the home of her childhood and lay her weary head upon her mother's bosom, to be folded again in her loving arms, to lay that poor, bruised and aching heart where it might beat and throb closely to the loved ones at home.

A kind welcome awaited her. All that love and tenderness could devise was done to bring the bloom to her cheek and the light to her eye; but it was all in vain; her's was a disease that no medicine could cure, no earthly balm would heal. It was a slow wasting of the vital forces, the sickness of the soul. The unkindness and neglect of her husband, lay like a leaden weight upon her heart, and slowly oozed way its life-drops.

And where was he that had won her love, and then cast it aside as a useless thing, who rifled her heart of its wealth and spread bitter ashes upon its broken altars? He was lingering away from her when the death-damps were gathering on her brow, when his name was trembling on her lips! lingering away! when she was watching his coming, though the death films were gathering before her eyes, and earthly things were fading from her vision.

"I think I hear him now," said the dying woman, "surely that is his step;" but the sound died away in the distance. Again she started from an uneasy slumber, "that is his voice! I am so glad he has come."

Tears gathered in the eyes of the sad watchers by that dying bed, for they knew that she was deceived. He had not returned. For her sake they wished his coming. Slowly the hours waned away, and then came the sad, soul-sickening thought that she was forgotten, forgotten in the last hour of human need, forgotten when the spirit, about to be dissolved, paused for the last time on the threshold of existence, a weary watcher at the gates of death.

"He has forgotten me," again she faintly murmured, and the last tears she would ever shed on earth sprung to her mournful eyes, and clasping her hands together in silent anguish, a few broken sentences issued from her pale and quivering lips. They were prayers for strength and earnest pleading for him who had desolated her young life, by turning its sunshine to shadows, its smiles to tears.

"He has forgotten me," she murmured again, "but I can bear it, the bitterness of death is passed, and soon I hope to exchange the shadows of death for the brightness of eternity, the rugged paths of life for the golden streets of glory, and the care and turmoils of earth for the peace and rest of heaven."

Her voice grew fainter and fainter, they saw the shadows that never deceive flit over her pale and faded face, and knew that the death angel waited to soothe their weary one to rest, to calm the throbbing of her bosom and cool the fever of her brain.

And amid the silent hush of their grief the freed spirit, refined through suffering, and brought into divine harmony through the spirit of the living Christ, passed over the dark waters of death as on a bridge of light, over whose radiant arches hovering angels bent. They parted the dark locks from her marble brow, closed the waxen lids over the once bright and laughing eye, and left her to the dreamless slumber of the grave.

Her cousin turned from that death-bed a sadder and wiser woman. She resolved more earnestly than ever to make the world better by her example, gladder by her presence, and to kindle the fires of her genius on the altars of universal love and truth. She had a higher and better object in all her writings than the mere acquisition of gold, or acquirement of fame.

She felt that she had a high and holy mission on the battle-field of existence, that life was not given her to be frittered away in nonsense, or wasted away in trifling pursuits. She would willingly espouse an unpopular cause but not an unrighteous one. In her the down-trodden slave found an earnest advocate; the flying fugitive remembered her kindness as he stepped cautiously through our Republic, to gain his freedom in a monarchial land, having broken the chains on which the rust of centuries had gathered.

Little children learned to name her with affection, the poor called her blessed, as she broke her bread to the pale lips of hunger. Her life was like a beautiful story, only it was clothed with the dignity of reality and invested with the sublimity of truth. True, she was an old maid.

No husband brightened her life with his love, or shaded it with his neglect. No children nestling lovingly in her arms called her mother. No one appended Mrs. to her name; she was indeed an old maid, not vainly striving to keep up an appearance of girlishness, when departed was written on her youth.

Not vainly pining at her loneliness and isolation: the world was full of warm, loving hearts, and her own beat in unison with them. Neither was she always sentimentally sighing for something to love, objects of affection were all around her, and the world was not so wealthy in love that it had no use for her's; in blessing others she made a life and benediction, and as old age descended peacefully and gently upon her, she had learned one of life's most precious lessons, that true happiness consists not so much in the fruition of our wishes as in the regulation of desires and the full development and right culture of our whole statures.

SKETCHES OF SOUTHERN LIFE

AUNT CHLOE

I REMEMBER, well remember,
    That dark and dreadful day,
When they whispered to me, "Chloe,
    Your children's sold away!"

It seemed as if a bullet
    Had shot me through and through,
And I felt as if my heart-strings
    Was breaking right in two.

And I says to cousin Milly,
    "There must be some mistake;
Where's Mistus?" "In the great house crying—
    Crying like her heart would break."

"And the lawyer's there with Mistus;
    Says he's come to 'ministrate,
'Cause when master died he just left
    Heap of debt on the estate."

"And I thought 'twould do you good
    To bid your boys good-bye—
To kiss them both and shake their hands,
    And have a hearty cry."

"Oh! Chloe, I knows how you feel,
    'Cause I'se been through it all;
I thought my poor old heart would break,
    When master sold my Saul."

Just then I heard the footsteps
    Of my children at the door,
And I rose right up to meet them,
    But I fell upon the floor.

And I heard poor Jakey saying,
  "Oh, mammy, don't you cry!"
And I felt my children kiss me
  And bid me, both, good-bye.

Then I had a mighty sorrow,
  Though I nursed it all alone;
But I wasted to a shadow,
  And turned to skin and bone.

But one day dear uncle Jacob
  (In heaven he's now a saint)
Said, "Your poor heart is in the fire,
  But child you must not faint."

Then I said to uncle Jacob,
  If I was good like you,
When the heavy trouble dashed me
  I'd know just what to do.

Then he said to me, "Poor Chloe,
  The way is open wide:"
And he told me of the Saviour,
  And the fountain in His side.

Then he said "Just take your burden
  To the blessed Master's feet;
I takes all my troubles, Chloe,
  Right unto the mercy-seat."

His words waked up my courage,
  And I began to pray,
And I felt my heavy burden
  Rolling like a stone away.

And a something seemed to tell me,
  You will see your boys again—
And that hope was like a poultice
  Spread upon a dreadful pain.

And it often seemed to whisper,
    Chloe, trust and never fear;
You'll get justice in the kingdom,
    If you do not get it here.

THE DELIVERANCE

Master only left old Mistus
    One bright and handsome boy;
But she fairly doted on him,
    He was her pride and joy.

We all liked Mister Thomas,
    He was so kind at heart;
And when the young folkes got in scrapes,
    He always took their part.

He kept right on that very way
    Till he got big and tall,
And old Mistus used to chide him,
    And say he'd spile us all.

But somehow the farm did prosper
    When he took things in hand;
And though all the servants liked him,
    He made them understand.

One evening Mister Thomas said,
    "Just bring my easy shoes:
I am going to sit by mother,
    And read her up the news."

Soon I heard him tell old Mistus
    "We're bound to have a fight;
But we'll whip the Yankees, mother,
    We'll whip them sure as night!"

Then I saw old Mistus tremble;
    She gasped and held her breath;
And she looked on Mister Thomas
    With a face as pale as death.

"They are firing on Fort Sumpter;
     Oh! I wish that I was there!—
Why, dear mother! what's the matter?
     You're the picture of despair."

"I was thinking, dearest Thomas,
     'Twould break my very heart
If a fierce and dreadful battle
     Should tear our lives apart."

"None but cowards, dearest mother,
     Would skulk unto the rear,
When the tyrant's hand is shaking
     All the heart is holding dear."

I felt sorry for old Mistus;
     She got too full to speak;
But I saw the great big tear-drops
     A running down her cheek.

Mister Thomas too was troubled
     With choosing on that night,
Betwixt staying with his mother
     And joining in the fight.

Soon down into the village came
     A call for volunteers;
Mistus gave up Mister Thomas,
     With many sighs and tears.

His uniform was real handsome;
     He looked so brave and strong;
But somehow I couldn't help thinking
     His fighting must be wrong.

Though the house was very lonesome,
     I thought 'twould all come right,
For I felt somehow or other
     We was mixed up in that fight.

And I said to Uncle Jacob,
    "Now old Mistus feels the sting,
For this parting with your children
    Is a mighty dreadful thing."

"Never mind," said Uncle Jacob,
    "Just wait and watch and pray,
For I feel right sure and certain,
    Slavery's bound to pass away;"

"Because" I asked the Spirit,
    "If God is good and just,
How it happened that the masters
    Did grind us to the dust."

"And something reasoned right inside,
    Such should not always be;
And you could not beat it out my head,
    The Spirit spoke to me."

And his dear old eyes would brighten,
    And his lips put on a smile,
Saying, "Pick up faith and courage,
    And just wait a little while."

Mistus prayed up in the parlor,
    That the Secesh all might win;
We were praying in the cabins,
    Wanting freedom to begin.

Mister Thomas wrote to Mistus,
    Telling 'bout the Bull's Run fight,
That his troops had whipped the Yankees
    And put them all to flight.

Mistus' eyes did fairly glisten;
    She laughed and praised the South,
But I thought some day she'd laugh
    On tother side her mouth.

I used to watch old Mistus' face,
    And when it looked quite long
I would say to Cousin Milly,
    The battle's going wrong;

Not for us, but for the Rebels.—
    My heart 'would fairly skip,
When Uncle Jacob used to say,
    "The North is bound to whip."

And let the fight go as it would—
    Let North or South prevail—
He always kept his courage up,
    And never let it fail.

And he often used to tell us,
    "Children, don't forget to pray;
For the darkest time of morning
    Is just 'fore the break of day."

Well, one morning bright and early
    We heard the fife and drum,
And the booming of the cannon—
    The Yankee troops had come.

When the word ran through the village,
    The colored folks are free—
In the kitchens and the cabins
    We held a jubilee.

When they told us Mister Lincoln
    Said that slavery was dead,
We just poured our prayers and blessings
    Upon his precious head.

We just laughed, and danced, and shouted,
    And prayed, and sang, and cried,
And we thought dear Uncle Jacob
    Would fairly crack his side.

But when old Mistus heard it,
    She groaned and hardly spoke;
When she had to lose her servants,
    Her heart was almost broke.

'Twas a sight to see our people
    Going out, the troops to meet,
Almost dancing to the music,
    And marching down the street.

After years of pain and parting,
    Our chains was broke in two,
And we was so mighty happy,
    We didn't know what to do.

But we soon got used to freedom,
    Though the way at first was rough;
But we weathered through the tempest,
    For slavery made us tough.

But we had one awful sorrow,
    It almost turned my head,
When a mean and wicked cretur
    Shot Mister Lincoln dead.

'Twas a dreadful solemn morning,
    I just staggered on my feet;
And the women they were crying
    And screaming in the street.

But if many prayers and blessings
    Could bear him to the throne,
I should think when Mister Lincoln died,
    That heaven just got its own.

Then we had another President,—
    What do you call his name?
Well, if the colored folks forget him
    They wouldn't be much to blame.

We thought he'd be the Moses
    Of all the colored race;
But when the Rebels pressed us hard
    He never showed his face.

But something must have happened him,
    Right curi's I'll be bound,
'Cause I heard 'em talking 'bout a circle
    That he was swinging round.

But everything will pass away—
    He went like time and tide—
And when the next election came
    They let poor Andy slide.

But now we have a President,
    And if I was a man
I'd vote for him for breaking up
    The wicked Ku-Klux Klan.

And if any man should ask me
    If I would sell my vote,
I'd tell him I was not the one
    To change and turn my coat;

If freedom seem'd a little rough
    I'd weather through the gale;
And as to buying up my vote,
    I hadn't it for sale.

I do not think I'd ever be
    As slack as Jonas Handy;
Because I heard he sold his vote
    For just three sticks of candy.

But when John Thomas Reeder brought
    His wife some flour and meat,
And told her he had sold his vote
    For something good to eat,

You ought to seen Aunt Kitty raise,
    And heard her blaze away;
She gave the meat and flour a toss,
    And said they should not stay.

And I should think he felt quite cheap
    For voting the wrong side;
And when Aunt Kitty scolded him,
    He just stood up and cried.

But the worst fooled man I ever saw,
    Was when poor David Rand
Sold out for flour and sugar;
    The sugar was mixed with sand.

I'll tell you how the thing got out;
    His wife had company,
And she thought the sand was sugar,
    And served it up for tea.

When David sipped and sipped the tea,
    Somehow it didn't taste right;
I guess when he found he was sipping sand,
    He was made enough to fight.

The sugar looked so nice and white—
    It was spread some inches deep—
But underneath was a lot of sand;
    Such sugar is mighty cheap.

You'd laughed to seen Lucinda Grange
    Upon her husband's track;
When he sold his vote for rations
    She made him take 'em back.

Day after day did Milly Green
    Just follow after Joe,
And told him if he voted wrong
    To take his rags and go.

I think that Curnel Johnson said
    His side had won the day,
Had not we women radicals
    Just got right in the way.

And yet I would not have you think
    That all our men are shabby;
But 'tis said in every flock of sheep
    There will be one that's scabby.

I've heard, before election came
    They tried to buy John Slade;
But he gave them all to understand
    That he wasn't in that trade.

And we've got lots of other men
    Who rally round the cause,
And go for holding up the hands
    That gave us equal laws

Who know their freedom cost too much
    Of blood and pain and treasure,
For them to fool away their votes
    For profit or for pleasure.

Aunt Chloe's Politics

Of course, I don't know very much
  About these politics,
But I think that some who run 'em,
  Do mighty ugly tricks.

I've seen 'em honey-fugle round,
  And talk so awful sweet,
That you'd think them full of kindness,
  As an egg is full of meat.

Now I don't believe in looking
  Honest people in the face,
And saying when you're doing wrong,
  That "I haven't sold my race."

When we want to school our children,
  If the money isn't there,
Whether black or white have took it,
  The loss we all must share.

And this buying up each other
  Is something worse than mean,
Though I thinks a heap of voting,
  I go for voting clean.

FRANCES ELLEN WATKINS HARPER

LEARNING TO READ

Very soon the Yankee teachers
    Came down and set up school;
But, oh! how the Rebs did hate it,—
    It was agin' their rule.

Our masters always tried to hide
    Book learning from our eyes;
Knowledge didn't agree with slavery—
    'Twould make us all too wise.

But some of us would try to steal
    A little from the book,
And put the words together,
    And learn by hook or crook.

I remember Uncle Caldwell,
    Who took pot liquor fat
And greased the pages of his book,
    And hid it in his hat.

And had his master ever seen
    The leaves upon his head,
He'd have thought them greasy papers,
    But nothing to be read.

And there was Mr. Turner's Ben,
    Who heard the children spell,
And picked the words right up by heart,
    And learned to read 'em well.

Well, the Northern folks kept sending
    The Yankee teachers down;
And they stood right up and helped us,
    Though Rebs did sneer and frown.

And, I longed to read my Bible,
    For precious words it said;
But when I begun to learn it,
    Folks just shook their heads,

And said there is no use trying,
    Oh! Chloe, you're too late;
But as I was rising sixty,
    I had no time to wait.

So I got a pair of glasses,
    And straight to work I went,
And never stopped till I could read
    The hymns and Testament.

Then I got a little cabin
    A place to call my own—
And I felt as independent
    As the queen upon her throne.

FRANCES ELLEN WATKINS HARPER

Church Building

Uncle Jacob often told us,
    Since freedom blessed our race
We ought all to come together
    And build a meeting place.

So we pinched, and scraped, and spared,
    A little here and there:
Though our wages was but scanty,
    The church did get a share.

And, when the house was finished,
    Uncle Jacob came to pray;
He was looking mighty feeble,
    And his head was awful gray.

But his voice rang like a trumpet;
    His eyes looked bright and young;
And it seemed a mighty power
    Was resting on his tongue.

And he gave us all his blessing—
    'Twas parting words he said,
For soon we got the message
    The dear old man was dead.

But I believe he's in the kingdom,
    For when we shook his hand
He said, "Children, you must meet me
    Right in the promised land;

For when I'm done a moiling
    And toiling here below,
Through the gate into the city
    Straightway I hope to go."

The Reunion

Well, one morning real early
    I was going down the street,
And I heard a stranger asking
    For Missis Chloe Fleet.

There was something in his voice
    That made me feel quite shaky,
And when I looked right in his face,
    Who should it be but Jakey!

I grasped him tight, and took him home—
    What gladness filled my cup!
And I laughed, and just rolled over,
    And laughed, and just give up.

"Where have you been? O Jakey, dear!
    Why didn't you come before?
Oh! when you children went away
    My heart was awful sore."

"Why, mammy, I've been on your hunt
    Since ever I've been free,
And I have heard from brother Ben,—
    He's down in Tennessee."

"He wrote me that he had a wife."
    "And children?" "Yes, he's three."
"You married, too?" "Oh no, indeed,
    I thought I'd first get free."

"Then, Jakey, you will stay with me,
    And comfort my poor heart;
Old Mistus got no power now
    To tear us both apart."

"I'm richer now than Mistus,
　　Because I have got my son;
And Mister Thomas he is dead,
　　And she's got nary one."

"You must write to brother Benny
　　That he must come this fall,
And we'll make the cabin bigger,
　　And that will hold us all."

"Tell him I want to see 'em all
　　Before my life do cease:
And then, like good old Simeon,
　　I hope to die in peace."

"I Thirst"

I Thirst, but earth cannot allay
    The fever coursing through my veins,
The healing stream is far away—
    It flows through Salem's lovely plains.

The murmurs of its crystal flow
    Break ever o'er this world of strife;
My heart is weary, let me go,
    To bathe it in the stream of life;

For many worn and weary hearts
    Have bathed in this pure healing stream,
And felt their griefs and cares depart,
    E'en like some sad forgotten dream.

"The Word is nigh thee, even in thy heart."

Say not, within thy weary heart,
    Who shall ascend above,
To bring unto thy fever'd lips
    The fount of joy and love.

Nor do thou seek to vainly delve
    Where death's pale angels tread,
To hear the murmur of its flow
    Around the silent dead.

Within, in thee is one living fount,
    Fed from the springs above;
There quench thy thirst till thou shalt bathe
    In God's own sea of love.

120   FRANCES ELLEN WATKINS HARPER

The Dying Queen

"I would meet death awake."

The strength that bore her on for years
    Was ebbing fast away,
And o'er the pale and life-worn face,
    Death's solemn shadows lay.

With tender love and gentle care,
    Friends gathered round her bed,
And for her sake each footfall hushed
    The echoes of its tread.

They knew the restlessness of death
    Through every nerve did creep,
And carefully they tried to lull
    The dying Queen to sleep.

In vain she felt Death's icy hand
    Her failing heart-strings shake;
And, rousing up, she firmly said,
    "I'd meet my God awake."

Awake, I've met the battle's shock,
    And born the cares of state;
Nor shall I take your lethean cup,
    And slumber at death's gate.

Did I not watch with eyes alert,
    The path where foes did tend;
And shall I veil my eyes with sleep,
    To meet my God and friend?

Nay, rather from my weary lids,
    This heavy slumber shake,
That I may pass the mystic vale,
    And meet my God awake.

The Jewish Grandfather's Story

Come, gather around me, children,
    And a story I will tell.
How we builded the beautiful temple—
    The temple we love so well.

I must date my story backward
    To a distant age and land,
When God did break our fathers' chains
    By his mighty outstretched hand

Our fathers were strangers and captives,
    Where the ancient Nile doth flow;
Smitten by cruel taskmasters,
    And burdened by toil and woe.

As a shepherd, to pasture green
    Doth lead with care his sheep,
So God divided the great Red Sea,
    And led them through the deep.

You've seen me plant a tender vine,
    And guard it with patient care,
Till its roots struck in the mellow earth,
    And it drank the light and air.

So God did plant our chosen race,
    As a vine in this fair land;
And we grew and spread a fruitful tree,
    The planting of his right hand.

The time would fail strove I to tell,
    All the story of our race—
Of our grand old leader, Moses,
    And Joshua in his place,

Of all our rulers and judges,
    From Joshua unto Saul,
Over whose doomed and guilty head
    Fell ruin and death's dark pall.

Of valiant Jepthath, whose brave heart
    With sudden grief did bow,
When his daughter came with dance and song
    Unconscious of his vow.

Of Gideon, lifting up his voice
    To him who rules the sky,
And wringing out his well drenched fleece,
    When all around was dry.

How Deborah, neath her spreading palms,
    A judge in Israel rose,
And wrested victory from the hands
    Of Jacob's heathen foes.

Of Samuel, an upright judge.
    The last who ruled our tribes,
Whose noble life and cleanly hands,
    Were pure and free from bribes.

Of David, with his checkered life
    Our tuneful minstrel king,
Who breathed in sadness and delight,
    The psalms we love to sing.

Of Solomon, whose wandering heart,
    From Jacob's God did stray,
And cast the richest gifts of life,
    In pleasure's cup away.

How aged men advised his son,
    But found him weak and vain,
Until the kingdom from his hands
    Was rudely rent in twain.

Oh! sin and strife are fearful things,
    They widen as they go,
And leave behind them shades of death,
    And open gates of woe.

A trail of guilt, a gloomy line,
    Ran through our nation's life,
And wicked kings provoked our God,
    And sin and woe were rife.

At length, there came a day of doom—
    A day of grief and dread;
When judgment like a fearful storm
    Swept o'er our country's head.

And we were captives many years,
    Where Babel's stream doth flow;
With harps unstrung, on willows hung,
    We wept in silent woe.

We could not sing the old, sweet songs,
    Our captors asked to hear;
Our hearts were full, how could we sing
    The songs to us so dear?

As one who dreams a mournful dream,
    Which fades, as wanes the night,
So God did change our gloomy lot
    From darkness into light.

Belshazzar in his regal halls,
    A sumptuous feast did hold;
He praised his gods and drank his wine
    From sacred cups of gold.

When dance and song and revelry
    Had filled with mirth each hall,
Belshazzar raised his eyes and saw
    A writing on the wall.

FRANCES ELLEN WATKINS HARPER

He saw, and horror blanched his cheek,
    His lips were white with fear;
To read the words he quickly called
    For wise men, far and near.

But baffled seers, with anxious doubt
    Stood silent in the room,
When Daniel came, a captive youth,
    And read the words of doom.

That night, within his regal hall,
    Belshazzar lifeless lay;
The Persians grasped his fallen crown,
    And with the Mede held sway.

Darius came, and Daniel rose
    A man of high renown;
But wicked courtiers schemed and planned
    To drag the prophet down.

They came as men who wished to place
    Great honors on their king—
With flattering lips and oily words,
    Desired a certain thing.

They knew that Daniel, day by day
    Towards Salem turned his face,
And asked the king to sign a law
    His hands might not erase.

That till one moon had waned away,
    No cherished wish or thing
Should any ask of men or Gods,
    Unless it were the king.

But Daniel, full of holy trust,
    His windows opened wide,
Regardless of the king's command,
    Unto his God he cried.

They brought him forth that he might be
    The hungry lion's meat,
Awe struck, the lions turned away
    And crouched anear his feet.

The God he served was strong to save
    His servant in the den;
The fate devised for Daniel's life
    O'er took those scheming men.

And Cyrus came, a gracious king,
    And gave the blest command,
That we, the scattered Jews, should build
    Anew our fallen land.

The men who hated Juda's weal
    Were filled with bitter rage,
And 'gainst the progress of our work
    Did evil men engage.

Sanballat tried to hinder us,
    And Gashmu uttered lies,
But like a thing of joy and light,
    We saw our temple rise.

And from the tower of Hananeel
    Unto the corner gate,
We built the wall and did restore
    The places desolate.

Some mocked us as we labored on
    And scoffingly did say,
"If but a fox climb on the wall,
    Their work will give away."

But Nehemiah wrought in hope,
    Though heathen foes did frown
"My work is great," he firmly said,
    "And I cannot come down."

FRANCES ELLEN WATKINS HARPER

And when Shemai counselled him
    The temple door to close,
To hide, lest he should fall a prey
    Unto his cruel foes.

Strong in his faith, he answered, "No,
    He would oppose the tide,
Should such as he from danger flee,
    And in the temple hide?"

We wrought in earnest faith and hope
    Until we built the wall,
And then, unto a joyful feast
    Did priest and people call.

We came to dedicate the wall
    With sacrifice and joy—
A happy throng, from aged sire
    Unto the fair-haired boy.

Our lips so used to mournful songs,
    Did joyous laughter fill,
And strong men wept with sacred joy
    To stand on Zion's hill.

Mid scoffing foes and evil men,
    We built our city blest,
And 'neath our sheltering vines and palms
    Today in peace we rest.

Shalmanezer, Prince of Cosman

Shalmanezer, Prince of Cosman, stood on the threshold of manly life, having just received a rich inheritance which had been left him by his father.

He was a magnificent-looking creature—the very incarnation of manly strength and beauty. The splendid poise of his limbs, the vigor and litheness of his motions, the glorious light that flashed from his splendid dark eyes, the bright joyous smiles that occasionally wreathed his fresh young lips, and the finely-erect carriage of his head, were enough to impress the beholder with the thought, "Here is an athlete armed for a glorious strife!"

While Shalmanezer was thinking upon his rich inheritance and how he should use it, he suddenly lifted his eyes and saw two strange-looking personages standing near him. They both advanced towards Shalmanezer when they saw their presence had attracted his attention.

The first one that approached the young man and addressed him, was named Desire. He was a pleasant-looking youth, with a flushed face, and eager, restless eyes. He looked as if he had been pursuing a journey, or had been grasping at an object he had failed to obtain. There was something in his manner that betrayed a want of rest—a look in his eyes which seemed to say, "I am not satisfied." But when he approached, he smiled in the most seductive manner, and, reaching out his hand to Shalmanezer said:

"I have come to welcome thee to man's estate, and for thy enjoyment, I have brought thee three friends who will lead thee into the brightest paths, and press to thy lips the sweetest elixirs."

Gladly the young man received the greeting of Desire, who immediately introduced his three companions, whose names were, Pleasure, Wealth, and Fame.—Pleasure was a most beautiful creature. Her lovely dark eyes flashed out a laughing light; upon her finely-carved lips hovered the brightest and sweetest smiles, which seemed ever ready to break into merry ripples of laughter; her robe was magnificently beautiful, as if it had imprisoned in its warp and woof the beauty of the rainbow and the glory of the setting sun; in her hand she held a richly wrought chalice in which sparkled and effervesced a ruby-colored liquid which was as beautiful to the eye as it was pleasant to the taste. When Pleasure was presented to Shalmanezer, she held out to him her cup and said in the sweetest tones:

> *"Come, drink of my cup. It is sparkling and bright*
> *As rubies distilled in the morning light;*
> *A truce to sorrow and adieu to pain—*
> *Here's the cup to strengthen, soothe and sustain."*

Just as Shalmanezer was about to grasp the cup, the other personage approached him. Her name was Peace, and she was attended by a mild, earnest-looking young man called Self Denial. In the calm depths of her dark-blue eyes was a tender, loving light, and on her brow a majestic serenity which seemed to say, "The cares of earth are at my feet; in vain its tempests sweep around my path." There was also a look of calm, grand patience on the brow of her attendant, which gave him the aspect of one who had passed through suffering unto Peace. Shalmanezer was gazing eagerly on the fair young face of Pleasure, and about to quaff the sparkling nectar, when Peace suddenly arrested his hand and exclaimed:

> *"Beware of this cup! 'Neath its ruddy glow,*
> *Is an undercurrent of shame and woe;*
> *'Neath its sparkling sheen so fair and bright,*
> *Are serpents that hiss, and adders that bite."*

The young man paused a moment, looked on the plain garb of Peace and then on the enchanting loveliness of Pleasure, and, pushing aside the hand of Peace with a scornful gesture, he said proudly and defiantly:

"I will follow Pleasure!"

Peace, thus repulsed, turned sadly away; and Self-Denial, wounded by Shalmanezer's rude rejection, bowed his head in silent sorrow and disappeared from the scene.

As Peace departed, Shalmanezer eagerly grasped the cup of Pleasure and pressed it to his lips, while she clasped her hand in his and said in a most charming manner, "Follow me;" and then he went willingly to the place where she dwelt.

As Shalmanezer approached the palace of Pleasure he heard the sweetest music rising on the air in magnificent swells or sinking in ravishing cadences; at his feet were springing the brightest and fairest flowers; the sweetest perfumes were bathing the air with the most exquisite fragrance; beautiful girls moved like visions of loveliness through the mazy dance; rare old wines sparkled on the festal board; the richest viands and most luscious fruits tempted the taste; and laughter, dance and song filled the air with varied delights. For a while Shalmanezer was enraptured with the palace of Pleasure. But soon he became weary of its gay confusion. The merry ripples of laughter lost their glad freshness; the once delightful music seemed to faint into strange monotones—whether the defect was in his ear or in the music he could not tell, but somehow it had ceased to gratify him; the constant flow of merry talk grew strangely distasteful to him; the pleasant viands began to pall upon his taste; at times he thought he detected a bitterness in the rare old wines which Pleasure ever and anon presented to his lips, and he turned wearily away from everything that had pleased his taste or had charmed and entranced his senses.

Shalmanezer sat moodily wishing that Desire would return and bring with him another attendant to whom he had been introduced when he had first clasped hands with Pleasure, and whose name was Wealth. While he was musing, he lifted up his eyes and saw Wealth and Desire standing at the door of his Boudoir, and near them he saw the sweet loving face of Peace, who was attended by Self Denial. Peace was about to approach him, but he repulsed her with an impatient frown, and turning to Desire he said:

"I have grown weary of Pleasure, and I wish to be introduced to the halls of Wealth."

Taller, graver and less fair was Wealth, than her younger sister, Pleasure. If the beauty of Pleasure could be compared to the vernal freshness of Spring—that of Wealth suggested the maturity of golden harvests, and ripe autumnal fruits. Like Pleasure, she was very richly attired; a magnificent velvet robe fell in graceful folds around her well-proportioned form; like prisms of captured light, the most beautiful jewels gleamed and flashed in her hair; a girdle of the finest and most exquisitely wrought gold was clasped around her waist; her necklace and bracelets were formed of the purest jewels and finest diamonds.— But there was something in her face which betokened a want which all her wealth could not supply. There was a mournful restlessness in her eye that at times seemed to border on the deepest sadness; and yet, there was something so alluring in her manner, so dazzling in her attire, and fascinating in her surroundings, that men would often sacrifice time, talent, energy, and even conscience and manhood, to secure her smiles and bask in her favor.

"Shalmanezer," said Desire to Wealth, "has grown weary of thy sister, Pleasure, and would fain dwell in thy stately halls. Is there aught to hinder him from being one of thy favored guests?"

"Nothing at all," said Wealth, smiling. "The rich inheritance left him by his father has been increasing in value, and I am glad that he was too wise to throw in Pleasure's cup life's richest gifts away."

With these words she reached out her jewelled hand to Shalmanezer and said, "Follow me!"

Weary of the halls of Pleasure, Shalmanezer gladly rose to follow Wealth. As he was leaving, he paused a moment to bid adieu to Pleasure. But she was so changed, that he did not recognize in the faded woman with the weary, listless manner, dull eyes and hollow cheeks, the enchanting girl, who, a few years before, had led him to her halls a welcome and delighted guest. All was so changed. It seemed more like a dream than a reality, that he had dwelt for years in what now seemed like a disenchanted palace. The banquet table was strewn with broken and tasteless fragments; the flowers had lost their fragrance and beauty, and lay in piles of scentless leaves; the soft sweet music had fainted into low breathed sighs, and silence reigned in the deserted halls where dance and revelry and song had wreathed with careless mirth the bright and fleeting hours.

"Come," said Wealth, "my Chariot waits thee at the door."

Without one pang of regret, Shalmanezer turned from the halls of Pleasure, to ride with Wealth in her magnificent chariot.

As they drove along, Wealth showed Shalmanezer the smoke rising from a thousand factories. Pausing a moment, she said:—"I superintend these works and here are my subjects."

Shalmanezer gazed on the colossal piles of brick and mortar, as those castles of industry met his eye. Just then the bell rang, and he saw issuing from amid the smoke and whir of machinery a sight that filled his soul with deep compassion.

There were pale, sad-looking women wending their way home to snatch some moment's rest, and an humble meal before returning to their tasks. There were weary-looking men, who seemed to be degenerating in mental strength and physical vigor. There were young children who looked as if the warm fresh currents of life in their veins had been touched with premature decay. And saddest of all—he saw young girls who looked as if they were rapidly changing from unsophisticated girlhood into over-ripe womanhood.

"Are these thy servants?" said Shalmanezer, sadly.

"These," said Wealth, "are my servants, but not my favorites. In dark mines—close factories—beneath low roofed huts—they dig the glittering jewels, and weave the webs of splendor and beauty with which I adorn my favorites. But I see that the sight pains thee. Let us pass on to fairer scenes."

Bending down to her finely-liveried coachman, she whispered in his ear, and in a few minutes the factories, with their smoke and din, were left behind. Beautiful lawns, lovely parks, and elegant residences rose before the pleased eyes of Shalmanezer; beautiful children sported on the lawns; lovely girls roamed in the parks; and the whole scene was a bright contrast to those he had left behind.

At length they rode up an avenue of stately trees, and stopped at the home of Wealth. "Here is my dwelling," she said, "enter and be my welcome guest."

Shalmanezer accepted the invitation, and entering, gazed with delighted wonder on the splendor and beauty of the place. On the walls hung most beautiful pictures surrounded by the richest frames—rare creations of the grand old masters; lovely statues suggested the idea of life strangely imprisoned in marble; velvet carpets sank pleasantly beneath his tread; elegant book cases, inlaid with ivory and pearl, held on the shelves the grand and noble productions of the monarchs of mind who still rule from their graves in the wide realms of thought and imagination. In her halls were sumptuous halls for feasting; delightful alcoves for thought and meditation; lovely little boudoirs for cozy chats with cherished friends. Even religion found costly bibles and splendidly embossed prayer books in the chambers of repose, where beneath the softened light of golden lamps, the children of Wealth sank to rest on beds of down.

"Surely," said Shalmanezer, "he must be a strangely restless creature, who cannot be satisfied in this home of beauty, grace and affluence." And yet, while he spake, he was conscious of a sense of unrest. He tried to shake it off, but still it would return. He would find himself sighing amid the fairest scenes—oppressed with a sense of longing for something he could not define. His eye was not satisfied with seeing, nor his ear with hearing. It seemed as if life had been presented to him as a luscious fruit, and he had eagerly extracted its richest juices, and was ready to throw away the bitter rind in hopeless disgust.

While he sat gloomily surveying the past, and feeling within his soul a hunger which neither Wealth nor Pleasure could appease, he lifted his eyes towards a distant mountain whose summit was crowned with perpetual snows, although a thousand sunbeams warmed and cheered the vale below. As he gazed, he saw a youth with a proud gait, buoyant step and flashing eye, climbing the mount. In his hand he held a beautifully embossed card, on which was written an invitation from Fame to climb her almost inaccessible heights and hear the sweetest music that ever ravished mortal ear. As the youth ascended the mount, Shalmanezer heard the shouts of applause which were wafted to the ears of the young man, who continued to climb with unabated ardor.

"Here," said Shalmanezer, "is a task worthy of my powers. I have wasted much of my time in the halls of Pleasure; I have grown weary of the stately palaces of Wealth; I will go forth and climb the heights of Fame, and find a welcome in the suncrowned palaces of Renown. O, the sight of that young man inspires my soul, and gives new tone and vigor to my life. I will not pause another moment to listen to the blandishments of Wealth. Instead of treading on these soft carpets, I will brace my soul to climb the rugged heights to gaze upon the fair face of Fame."

Just as he was making this resolve, he saw Peace and her attendant gazing anxiously and silently upon him. His face flushed with sudden anger; a wrathful light flashed from his eyes; and turning his face coldly from Peace, he said: "I do wish Peace would come without her unwelcome companion—Self-Denial I do utterly and bitterly hate." Peace again repulsed, turned sadly away, followed by Self-Denial. With eager haste Shalmanezer rose up and left the bowers of Ease and halls of Pride, to tread the rugged heights of Fame, with patient, ready feet. As he passed upwards, new vigor braced his nerves. He felt an exhilaration of spirits he had never enjoyed in the halls of Wealth or bowers of Pleasure. Onward and upward he proudly moved, as the multitude, who stood at the base, cheered him with rapturous applause, and no music was ever so sweet to his ear as the plaudits of the crowd; but, as he ascended higher and higher, the voices of the multitude grew fainter and fainter; some voices that cheered him at the beginning of his journey had melted into the stillness of death; others had harshened into the rough tones of disapprobation; others were vociferously applauding a new aspirant who had since started to climb the summit of Renown; but, with his eye upon the palace of Fame, he still climbed on, while the air grew rarer, and the atmosphere colder. The old elasticity departed from his limbs, and the buoyancy from his spirits, and it seemed as if the chills of death were slowly creeping around his heart. But still, with fainter step he kept climbing upward, until almost exhausted, he sank down at the palace-gate of Fame, exclaiming, "Is this all?"

Very stately and grand was the cloud-capped palace of Fame. The pillars of her lofty abode were engraven with the names of successful generals, mighty conquerors, great leaders, grand poets, illustrious men and celebrated women. There were statues on which the tooth of Time was slowly gnawing; the statues of men whose brows had once been surrounded by a halo of glory, but were now darkened by the shadow of their crimes. Those heights which had seemed so enchanting at a distance, now seemed more like barren mounds, around which the chills of Death were ever sweeping.

Fame heard the voice of her votary, and came out to place upon his brow her greenest bays and brightest laurels, and bid him welcome to her palace; but when she saw the deathly whiteness of his face, she shrank back in pity and fear. The light was fading from his eye; his limbs had lost their manly strength; and Fame feared that the torpor of Death would overtake him before she could crown him as her honored guest. She bent down her ear to the sufferer, and heard him whisper slowly, "Peace! Peace!"

Then said Fame to her servants, "Descend to the vale, bring the best medical skill ye can find, and search for Peace, and entreat her to come; tell her that one of my votaries lies near to death, and longs for her presence." The servants descended to the vale, and soon returned, bringing with them a celebrated physician.—Peace had heard the cry of Shalmanezer, and had entered the room with her companion before the doctor had come. When the physician saw Shalmanezer, he gazed anxiously upon him, felt the fluttering pulse, and chafed the pale cold hands to restore the warmth and circulation.

In the meantime, Pleasure and Wealth having heard the story of Shalmanezer's illness, entered the room. "There is but one thing," said the physician, "can save Shalmanezer's life: some one must take the warm healthy blood from his veins and inject it into Shalmanezer's veins before he can be restored to health."

Pleasure and Wealth looked aghast when they heard the doctor's prescription. Pleasure suddenly remembered that she had a pressing engagement; Wealth said "I am no longer young, nor even well, and am sure I have not one drop of blood to spare;" Fame pitied her faithful votary, but amid the cold blasts that swept around her home, was sure it would be very imprudent for her to attempt to part with so much blood.

FRANCES ELLEN WATKINS HARPER

Just as Pleasure, Wealth and Fame had refused to give the needed aid, Desire entered the room, but when he heard the conditions for the restoration of Shalmanezer, shrank back in selfish dismay, and refused also.

As Shalmanezer lay gasping for breath, and looking wistfully at his old companions, Peace, attended by Self-Denial, drew near the sick man's couch. Shalmanezer opened his eyes languidly, and closed them wearily; when life was like a joyous dream, he had repulsed Peace and utterly hated Self Denial, and what could he dare hope from either in his hour of dire extremity. While he lay with his eyes half-closed, Self Denial approached the bedside, and baring his arm, said to the doctor:

"Here is thy needed remedy. Take the blood from these veins, and with it restore Shalmanezer to health and strength."

The doctor struck his lancet into Self-Denial's arm, and drawing from it the needed quantity of blood, injected it into Shalmanezer's veins. The remedy was effectual. Health flushed the cheeks of Shalmanezer, and braced each nerve with new vigor, and he soon recovered from his fearful exhaustion. Then his heart did cleave unto Self-Denial. He had won his heart by his lofty sacrifice. He had bought his love by the blood from his own veins. Clasping hands with Self-Denial, he trod with him the paths of Peace, and in so doing, received an amount of true happiness which neither Pleasure, Wealth nor Fame could give.

Out in the Cold

Out in the cold mid the dreary night,
Under the eaves of homes so bright:
Snowflakes falling o'er mother's grave
Will no one rescue, no one save?

A child left out in the dark and cold,
A lamb not sheltered in any fold,
Hearing the wolves of hunger bark,
Out in the cold! and out in the dark

Missing tonight the charming bliss,
That lies in the mother's good-night kiss;
And hearing no loving father's prayer,
For blessings his children all may share.

Creeping away to some wretched den,
To sleep mid the curses of drunken men
And women, not as God has made,
Wrecked and ruined, wronged and betrayed.

Church of the Lord reach out thy arm,
And shield the hapless one from harm;
Where the waves of sin are dashing wild
Rescue and save the drifting child.

Wash from her life guilt's turbid foam,
In the fair haven of a home;
Tenderly lead the motherless girl
Up to the gates of purest pearl.

The wandering feet which else had strayed,
From thorny paths may yet be stayed;
And a crimson track through the cold dark night
May exchange to a line of loving light.

Save the Boys

Like Dives in the deeps of Hell
I cannot break this fearful spell,
Nor quench the fires I've madly nursed,
Nor cool this dreadful raging thirst.
Take back your pledge—ye come too late!
Ye cannot save me from my fate,
Nor bring me back departed joys;
But ye can try to save the boys.

Ye bid me break my fiery chain,
Arise and be a man again,
When every street with snares is spread,
And nets of sin where'er I tread.
No; I must reap as I did sow.
The seeds of sin bring crops of woe;
But with my latest breath I'll crave
That ye will try the boys to save.

These bloodshot eyes were once so bright;
This sin-crushed heart was glad and light;
But by the wine-cup's ruddy glow
I traced a path to shame and woe.
A captive to my galling chain,
I've tried to rise, but tried in vain—
The cup allures and then destroys.
Oh! from its thraldom save the boys.

Take from your streets those traps of hell
Into whose gilded snares I fell.
Oh! freemen, from these foul decoys
Arise, and vote to save the boys.
Oh ye who license men to trade
In draughts that charm and then degrade,
Before ye hear the cry, Too late,
Oh, save the boys from my sad fate.

Nothing and Something

It is nothing to me, the beauty said,
With a careless toss of her pretty head;
The man is weak if he can't refrain
From the cup you say is fraught with pain.
It was something to her in after years;
When her eyes were drenched with burning tears,
And she watched in lonely grief and dread,
And startled to hear a staggering tread.

It is nothing to me, the mother said;
I have no fear that my boy will tread
In the downward path of sin and shame,
And crush my heart and darken his name.
It was something to her when that only son
From the path of right was early won,
And madly cast in the flowing bowl
A ruined body and sin-wrecked soul.

It is nothing to me, the young man cried:
In his eye was a flash of scorn and pride;
I heed not the dreadful things ye tell:
I can rule myself I know full well.
It was something to him when in prison he lay
The victim of drink, life ebbing away;
And thought of his wretched child and wife,
And the mournful wreck of his wasted life.

It is nothing to me, the merchant said,
As over his ledger he bent his head;
I'm busy today with tare and tret,
And I have no time to fume and fret.
It was something to him when over the wire
A message came from a funeral pyre—
A drunken conductor had wrecked a train,
And his wife and child were among the slain.

It is nothing to me, the voter said,
The party's loss is my greatest dread;
Then gave his vote for the liquor trade,
Though hearts were crushed and drunkards made.
It was something to him in after life,
When his daughter became a drunkard's wife
And her hungry children cried for bread,
And trembled to hear their father's tread.

Is it nothing for us to idly sleep
While the cohorts of death their vigils keep?
To gather the young and thoughtless in
And grind in our midst a grist of sin?
It is something, yes, all, for us to stand
Clasping by faith our Saviour's hand;
To learn to labor, live and fight
On the side of God and changeless light.

Wanderer's Return

My home is so glad, my heart is so light,
My wandering boy has returned tonight.
He is blighted and bruised, I know, by sin,
But I am so glad to welcome him in.

The child of my tenderest love and care
Has broken away from the tempter's snare;
Tonight my heart is o'erflowing with joy,
I have found again my wandering boy.

My heart has been wrung with a thousand fears,
Mine eyes have been drenched with the bitterest tears;
Like shadows that fade are my past alarms,
My boy is enclasped in his mother's arms.

The streets were not safe for my darling child;
Where sin with its evil attractions smiled.
But his wandering feet have ceased to roam,
And tonight my wayward boy is at home—

At home with the mother that loves him best,
With the hearts that have ached with sad unrest,
With the hearts that are thrilling with untold joy
Because we have found our wandering boy.

In that wretched man so haggard and wild
I only behold my returning child,
And the blissful tears from my eyes that start
Are the overflow of a happy heart.

I have trodden the streets in lonely grief,
I have sought in prayer for my sole relief;
But the depths of my heart tonight are stirred,
I know that the mother's prayer has been heard.

FRANCES ELLEN WATKINS HARPER

If the mother-love be so strong and great
For her child, sin-weary and desolate,
Oh what must the love of the Father be
For souls who have wandered like you and me!

"Fishers of Men"

I had a dream, a varied dream:
    Before my ravished sight
The city of my Lord arose,
    With all its love and light.

The music of a myriad harps
    Flowed out with sweet accord;
And saints were casting down their crowns
    In homage to our Lord.

My heart leaped up with untold joy;
    Life's toil and pain were o'er;
My weary feet at last had found
    The bright and restful shore.

Just as I reached the gates of light,
    Ready to enter in,
From earth arose a fearful cry
    Of sorrow and of sin.

I turned, and saw behind me surge
    A wild and stormy sea;
And drowning men were reaching out
    Imploring hands to me.

And ev'ry lip was blanched with dread
    And moaning for relief;
The music of the golden harps
    Grew fainter for their grief.

Let me return, I quickly said,
    Close to the pearly gate;
My work is with these wretched ones,
    So wrecked and desolate.

An angel smiled and gently said:
    This is the gate of life,
Wilt thou return to earth's sad scenes,
    Its weariness and strife,

To comfort hearts that sigh and break,
    To dry the falling tear,
Wilt thou forego the music sweet
    Entrancing now thy ear?

I must return, I firmly said,
    The strugglers in that sea
Shall not reach out beseeching hands
    In vain for help to me.

I turned to go; but as I turned
    The gloomy sea grew bright,
And from my heart there seemed to flow
    Ten thousand cords of light.

And sin-wrecked men, with eager hands,
    Did grasp each golden cord;
And with my heart I drew them on
    To see my gracious Lord.

Again I stood beside the gate.
    My heart was glad and free;
For with me stood a rescued throng
    The Lord had given me.

Signing the Pledge

Do you see this cup—this tempting cup—
    Its sparkle and its glow?
I tell you this cup has brought to me
    A world of shame and woe.

Do you see that woman sad and wan?
    One day with joy and pride,
With orange blossoms in her hair,
    I claimed her as my bride.

And vowed that I would faithful prove
    Till death our lives should part;
I've drenched her soul with floods of grief,
    And almost crushed her heart.

Do you see that gray-haired mother bend
    Beneath her weight of years?
I've filled that aged mother's eyes
    With many bitter tears.

Year after year for me she prays,
    And tries her child to save;
I've almost brought her gray hairs down
    In sorrow to the grave.

Do you see that boy whose wistful eyes
    Are gazing on my face?
I've overshadowed his young life
    With sorrow and disgrace.

He used to greet me with a smile,
    His heart was light and glad;
I've seen him tremble at my voice,
    I've made that heart so sad.

FRANCES ELLEN WATKINS HARPER

Do you see this pledge I've signed tonight?
    My mother, wife, and boy
Shall read my purpose on that pledge
    And smile through tears of joy.

To know this night, this very night,
    I cast the wine-cup down,
And from the dust of a sinful life
    Lift up my manhood's crown.

The faded face of my young wife
    With roses yet shall bloom,
And joy shall light my mother's eyes
    On the margin of the tomb.

I have vowed tonight my only boy,
    With brow so fair and mile,
Shall not be taunted on the streets,
    And called a drunkard's child.

Never again shall that young face
    Whiten with grief and dread,
Because I've madly staggered home
    And sold for drink his bread.

This strong right arm unnerved by rum
    Shall battle with my fate;
And peace and comfort crown the home
    By drink made desolate.

Like a drowning man, tempest-tossed,
    Clings to a rocky ledge,
With trembling hands I've learned to grasp
    The gospel and the pledge.

A captive bounding from my chain,
    I've rent each hateful band,
And by the help of grace divine
    A victor hope to stand.

LIGHT BEYOND THE DARKNESS

A FAIRER HOPE, A BRIGHTER MORN

From the peaceful heights of a higher life
I heard your maddening cry of strife
It quivered with anguish, wrath and pain,
Like a demon struggling with his chain.
A chain of evil, heavy and strong,
Rusted with ages of fearful wrong.
Encrusted with blood and burning tears.
The chain I had worn and dragged for years.
It clasped ray limbs, but it bound your heart.
And formed of your life a fearful part
You sowed the wind, but could not control
The tempest wild of a guilty soul.
You saw me stand with my broken chain
Forged in the furnace of fiery pain.
You saw my children around me stand
Lovingly clasping my unbound hand.
But you remembered my blood and tears
'Mid the weary wasting flight of years.
You thought of the rice swamps, lone and dank,
When my heart in hopeless anguish sank.
You thought of your fields with harvest white,
Where I toiled in paiu from morn till night
You thought of the days you bought and sold
The children I loved, for paltry gold.
You thought of our shrieks that rent the air—
Our moans of anguish and deep despair;
With chattering teeth and paling face,
You thought of your nation's deep disgrace,
You wove from your fears a fearful fate
To spring from your seeds of scorn and hate
You imagined the saddest, wildest thing,
That time, with revenges fierce, could bring
The cry you thought from a Voodoo breast
Was the echo of your soul's unrest;
When thoughts too sad for fruitless tears
Loomed like the ghosts of avenging years.

Oh, prophet of evil, could not your voice
In our new hopes and freedom rejoice?
'Mid the light which streams around our way
Was there naught to see but an evil day?
Nothing but vengeance, wrath and hate,
And the serpent coils of an evil fate—
A fate that shall crush and drag you down;
A doom that shall press like an iron crown?
A fate that shall crisp and curl your hair
And darken your faces now so fair.
And send through your veins like a poisoned flood
The hated stream of the Negro's blood?
A fate to madden the heart and brain
You've peopled with phantoms of dread and pain,
And fancies wild of your daughter's shriek
With Congo kisses upon her cheek?
Beyond the mist of your gloomy fears,
I see the promise of brighter years.
Through the dark I see their golden hem
And my heart gives out its glad amen.
The banner of Christ was your sacred trust.
But you trailed that banner in the dust,
And mockingly told us amid our pain
The hand of your God had forged our chain.
We stumbled and groped through the dreary night
Till our fingers touched God's robe of light;
And we knew He heard, from his lofty throne,
Our saddest cries and faintest moan.
The cross you have covered with sin and shame
We'll bear aloft in Christ's holy name.
Oh, never again may its folds be furled
While sorrow and sin enshroud our world
God, to whose fingers thrills each heart beat,
Has not sent us to walk with aimless feet,
To cower and crouch, with bated breath
From margins of life to shores of death.
Higher and better than hate for hate.
Like the scorpion fangs that desolate,
Is the hope of a brighter, fairer morn

FRANCES ELLEN WATKINS HARPER

And a peace and a love that shall yet be born;
When the Negro shall hold an honored place,
The friend and helper of every race;
His mission to build and not destroy.
And gladden the world with love and joy.

Our Hero

Onward to her destination,
O'er the stream the Hannah sped,
When a cry of consternation
Smote and chilled our hearts with dread.
Wildly leaping, madly sweeping,
All relentless in their sway,
Like a band of cruel demons.
Flames were closing 'round our way.
Oh! the horror of those moments;
Flames above and waves below.
Oh! the agony of ages
Crowded in one hour of woe.
Fainter grew our hearts with anguish
In that hour with peril rife,
When we saw the pilot flying,
Terror-stricken, for his life.
Then a man uprose before us—
We had once despised his race—
But we saw a lofty purpose
Lighting up his darkened face.
While the flames were madly roaring,
With a courage grand and high,
Forth he rushed unto our rescue,
Strong to suffer, brave to die.
Helplessly the boat was drifting,
Death was staring in each face,
When he grasped the fallen rudder.
Took the pilot's vacant place.
Could he save us? Would he save us
All his hope of life give o'er
Could he hold that fated vessel
Till she reached the nearer shore
All our hopes and fears were centred
'Round his strong, unfaltering hand;
If he failed us we must perish,
Perish just in sight of land.

FRANCES ELLEN WATKINS HARPER

Breathlessly we watched and waited
While the flames were raging fast
When our anguish changed to rapture—
We were saved, yes, saved at last.
Never strains of sweetest music
Brought to us more welcome sound
Than the grating of that steamer
When her keel had touched the ground.
But our faithful martyr hero
Through a fiery pathway trod,
Till he laid his valiant spirit
On the bosom of his God.
Fame has never crowned a hero
On the crimson fields of strife,
Grander, nobler, than that pilot
Yielding up for us his life.

Enlightened Motherhood: An Address

Before the Brooklyn Literary Society,
November 15th, 1892

It is nearly thirty years since an emancipated people stood on the threshold of a new era, facing an uncertain future—a legally un married race, to be taught the sacredness of the marriage relation; an ignorant people, to be taught to read the hook of the Christian law and to learn to comprehend more fully the claims of the gospel of the Christ of Calvary. A homeless race, to be gathered into homes of peaceful security and to he instructed how to plant around their firesides the strongest batteries against the sins that degrade and the race vices that demoralize. A race unversed in the science of government and unskilled in the just administration of law, to be translated from the old oligarchy of slavery into the new common wealth of freedom, and to whose men came the right to exchange the fetters on their wrists for the ballots in their right hands—a ballot which, if not vitiated by fraud or restrained by intimidation, counts just as much as that of the most talented and influential man in the land.

While politicians may stumble on the barren mountain of fretful controversy, and men, lacking faith in God and the invisible forces which make for righteousness, may shrink from the unsolved problems of the hour, into the hands of Christian women comes the opportunity of serving the ever blessed Christ, by ministering to His little ones and striving to make their homes the brightest spots on earth and the fairest types of heaven. The school may instruct and the church may teach, but the home is an institution older than the church and antedates school, and that is the place where children should be trained for useful citizenship on earth and a hope of holy companionship in heaven.

Every mother should endeavor to be a true artist. I do not mean by this that every woman should be a painter, sculptor, musician, poet, or writer, but the artist who will write on the tablet of childish innocence thoughts she will not blush to see read in the light of eternity and printed amid the archives of heaven, that the young may learn to wear them as amulets around their hearts and throw them as bulwarks around their lives, and that in the hour of temptation and trial the voices from home may linger around their paths as angels of guidance, around their steps, and be incentives to deeds of high and holy worth.

The home may be a humble spot, where there are no velvet carpets to hush your tread, no magnificence to surround your way, nor costly creations of painter's art or sculptor's skill to please your conceptions or gratify your tastes; but what are the costliest gifts of fortune when placed in the balance with the confiding love of dear children or the true devotion of a noble and manly husband whose heart can safely trust in his wife? You may place upon the brow of a true wife and mother the greenest laurels; you may crowd her hands with civic honors; but, after all, to her there will be no place like home, and the crown of her mother hood will be more precious than the diadem of a queen.

As marriage is the mother of homes, it is important that the duties and responsibilities of this relation should be understood before it is entered on. A mistake made here may run through every avenue of the future, cast its shadow over all our coming years, and enter the lives of those whom we should shield with our love and defend with our care. We may be versed in ancient lore and modern learning, may be able to trace the path of worlds that roll in light and power on high, and to tell when comets shall cast their trail over our evening skies. We may understand the laws of stratification well enough to judge where lies the vein of silver and where nature has hidden her virgin gold. We may be able to tell the story of departed nations and conquering chieftains who have added pages of tears and blood to the world's history; but our education is deficient if we are perfectly ignorant how to guide the little feet that are springing up so gladly in our path, and to see in undeveloped possibilities gold more fine than the pavements of heaven and gems more precious than the foundations of the holy city. Marriage should not be a blind rushing together of tastes and fancies, a mere union of fortunes or an affair of convenience. It should be a "tie that only love and truth should weave and nothing but death should part."

Marriage between two youthful and loving hearts means the laying the foundation stones of a new home, and the woman who helps erect that home should be careful not to build it above the reeling brain of a drunkard or the weakened fibre of a debauchee.

If it be folly for a merchant to send an argosy, laden with the richest treasures, at midnight on a moonless sea, without a rudder, compass, or guide, is it not madness for' a woman to trust her future happiness, and the welfare of the dear children who may yet nestle in her arms and make music and sunshine around her fireside, in the unsteady hands of a characterless man, too lacking in self-respect and self-control to hold the helm and rudder of his own life; who drifts where he ought to steer, and only lasts when he ought to live?

The moment the crown of motherhood falls on the brow of a young wife, God gives her a new interest in the welfare of the home and the good of society. If hitherto she had been content to trip through life a lighthearted girl, or to tread amid the halls of wealth and fashion the gayest of the gay, life holds for her now a high and noble service. She must be more than the child of pleasure or the devotee of fashion. Her work is grandly constructive. A helpless and ignorant babe lies smiling in her arms. God has trusted her with a child, and it is her privilege to help that child develop the most precious thing a man or woman can possess on earth, and that is a good character. Moth may devour our finest garments, fire may consume and floods destroy our fairest homes, rust may gather on our silver and tarnish our gold, but there is an asbestos that no fire can destroy, a treasure which shall be richer for its service and better for its use, and that is a good character.

But the question arises, What constitutes an enlightened motherhood I do not pretend that I will give you an exhaustive analysis of all that a mother should learn and of all she should teach. In the Christian scriptures the story is told of a mother of whom it was said: "From henceforth all nations shall call her blessed." While, in these days of religious unrest, criticism, and investigation, numbers are ready to relegate this story to the limbo of myth and fiction; whether that story be regarded as fact or fiction, there are lessons in it which we could not take into our lives without its making life higher, better, and more grandly significant. It is the teaching of a divine overshadowing and a touching self-surrender which still floats down the ages, fragrant with the aroma of a sweet submission. "The handmaid of the Lord, be it done unto me according to Thy word."

We read that Christ left us an example that we should tread in His footsteps; but does not the majority of the Christian world hold it as a sacred creed that the first print of His feet in the flesh began in the days of His antenatal life; and is not the same spirit in the world now which was there when our Lord made His advent among us, bone of our bone and flesh of our flesh; and do we not need the incarnation of God's love and light in our hearts as much now as it was ever needed in any preceding generation? Do we not need to hold it as a sacred thing, amid sorrow, pain, and wrong, that only through the love of God are human hearts made strong? And has not every prospective mother the right to ask for the overshadowing of the same spirit, that her child may be one of whom it may be truly said, "Of such is the kingdom of heaven," and all his life he shall be lent to the Lord Had all the mothers of this present generation dwelt beneath the shadow of the Almighty, would it have been possible for slavery to have cursed us with its crimes, or intemperance degraded us with its vices? Would the social evil still have power to send to our streets women whose laughter is sadder than their tears, and over whose wasted lives death draws the curtains of the grave and silently hides their sin and shame? Are there not women, respectable women, who feel that it would wring their hearts with untold anguish, and bring their gray hairs in sorrow to the grave, if their daughters should trail the robes of their womanhood in the dust, yet who would say of their sons, if they were trampling their manhood down and fettering their souls with cords of vice, "O, well, boys will be boys, and young men will sow their wild oats."

I hold that no woman loves social purity as it deserves to be loved and valued, if she cares for the purity of her daughters and not her sons who would gather her dainty robes from contact with the fallen woman and yet greet with smiling lips and clasp with warm and welcoming hands the author of her wrong and ruin. How many mothers today shrink from a double standard for society which can ostracise the woman and condone the offense of the man? How many mothers say within their hearts, I intend to teach my boy to be as pure in his life, as chaste in his conversation, as the young girl who sits at my side encircled in the warm clasp of loving arms? How many mothers strive to have their boys shun the gilded saloon as they would the den of a deadly serpent Not the mother who thoughtlessly sends her child to the saloon for a beverage to make merry with her friends. How many mothers teach their boys to shrink in horror from the fascinations of women, not as God made them, but as sin has degraded them?

Tonight, if you and I could walk through the wards of various hospitals at home and abroad, perhaps we would find hundreds, it may be thousands, of young men awaiting death as physical wrecks, having burned the candle of their lives at both ends. Were we to bend over their dying couches with pitying glances, and question them of their lives, perhaps numbers of them could tell you sad stories of careless words from thoughtless lips, that tainted their imaginations and sent their virus through their lives; of young eyes, above which God has made the heavens so eloquent with His praise, and the earth around so poetic with His ideas, turning from the splendor of the magnificent sunsets or glorious early dawns, and finding allurement in the dreadful fascinations of sin, or learning to gloat over impure pictures and vile literature. Then, later on, perhaps many of them could say, "The first time I went to a house where there were revelry and song, and the dead were there and I knew it not, I went with men who were older than myself; men, who should have showed me how to avoid the pitfalls which lie in the path of the young, the tempted, and inexperienced, taught me to gather the flowers of sin that blossom around the borders of hell."

Suppose we dared to question a little further, not from idle curiosity, but for the sake of getting, from the dying, object lessons for the living, and say, "God gave you, an ignorant child, into the hands of a mother. Did she never warn you of your dangers and teach you how to avoid them?" How many could truthfully say, "My mother was wise enough to teach me and faithful enough to warn me." If the cholera or yellow-fever were raging in any part of this city, and to enter that section meant peril to health and life, what mother would permit her child to walk carelessly through a district where pestilence was breathing its bane upon the morning air and distilling its poison upon the midnight dews? And yet, when boys go from the fireside into the arena of life, how many ever go there forewarned and forearmed against the soft seductions of vice, against moral conditions which are worse than "fever, plague and palsy, and madness *all* combined?"

Among the things I would present for the enlightenment of mothers are attention to the laws of heredity and environment. Mrs. Winslow, in a paper on social purity, speaks of a package of letters she had received from a young man of talent, good education, and a strong desire to live a pure and useful life. In boyhood he ignorantly ruined his health, and, when he resolved to rise above his depressed condition, his own folly, his heredity and environment, weighed him down like an incubus. His appeals, she says, are most touching. He says: "If you cannot help me, what can I do? My mother cursed me with illegitimacy and hereditary insanity. I have left only the alternative of suicide or madness." A fearful legacy! For stolen money and slandered character we may make reparation, but the opportunity of putting the right stamp on an antenatal life, if once gone, is gone forever; and there never was an angel of God, however bright, terrible, or strong he may be who was ever strong enough to roll away the stone from the grave of a dead opportunity.

In the annals of this State may be found a record of six generations of debased manhood and womanhood, and prominent among them stands the name of Margaret, the mother of criminals. She is reported as having five sisters, the greater number of whom trailed the robes of their womanhood in the dust, and became fallen women. Some time since, their posterity was traced out, and five hundred and forty persons are represented as sharing the blood of these unfortunate women; and it is remarkable, as well as very sad, to see the lines of debasement and weakness, vice and crime, which are displayed in their record. In the generation of Margaret, fifty percent, of the women were placed among the fallen, and in all the generations succeeding, including only those of twelve years of age and over, to the extent of fifty percent; and of this trail of weakness there were three families in the sixth generation who had six children sent to the house of refuge. Out of seven hundred and nine members of this family, nearly one-ninth have been criminals, and nearly one-tenth paupers; twenty-two had acquired property, and eight had lost property nearly one-seventh were illegitimate, and one sister was the mother of distinctively pauperized lines.

Or, take another line of thought. Would it not be well for us women to introduce into all of our literary circles, for the purpose of gaining knowledge, topics on this subject of heredity and the influence of good and bad conditions upon the home life of the race, and study this subject in the light of science for our own and the benefit of others? For instance, may we not seriously ask the question, Can a mother or father be an habitual tippler, or break God's law of social purity, and yet impart to their children, at the same time, abundant physical vitality and strong moral fibre? Can a father dash away the reins of moral restraint, and, at the same time, impart strong will-power to his offspring?

A generation since, there lived in a Western city a wealthy English gentleman who was what is called a high liver. He drank his toddy in the morning, washed down his lunch with champagne, and finished a bottle of port for dinner, though he complained that the heavy wines here did not agree with him, owing to the climate. He died of gout at fifty years, leaving four sons. One of them became an epileptic, two died from drinking. Called good fellows, generous, witty, honorable young men, but before middle age miserable sots. The oldest of the brothers was a man of fixed habits, occupying a leading place in the community, from his keen intelligence, integrity, and irreproachable morals. He watched over his brothers, laid them in their graves, and never ceased to denounce the vice which had ruined them; and when he was long past middle age, financial trouble threw him into a low, nervous condition, for which wine was prescribed. He drank but one bottle. Shortly after, his affairs were righted and his health and spirits returned, but it was observed that once or twice a year he mysteriously disappeared for a month or six weeks. Nor wife, nor children, nor even his partner, knew where he went; but at last, when he was old and gray headed, his wife was telegraphed from an obscure neighboring village, where she found him dying of *mania a potu*. He had been in the habit of hiding there when the desire for liquor became maddening, and when there he drank like a brute.

May Wright Sewall, president of the Woman's National Council, writing of disinherited children, tells of a country school where health and joyousnesss and purity were the rule, vulgarity and coarseness the exception, and morbid and mysterious manners quite unknown. There came one morning, in her childhood, two little girls, sisters, of ten and twelve years. They were comfortably dressed. At the noon day meal their baskets opened to an abundant and appetizing lunch. But they were not like other children. They had thin, pinched faces, with vulgar mouths, and a sidelong look from their always downcast eyes which made her shudder; and skin, so wrinkled and yellow, that her childish fears fancied them to be witches' children. They held themselves aloof from all the rest. For two or three years they sat in the same places in that quiet school doing very little work, but, not being disorderly, they were allowed to stay. One day, when my father had visited the school, as we walked home together, I questioned him as to what made Annie and Minnie so different from all the other little girls at the school, and the grave man answered: Before they were born their father sold their birthright, and they must feed on pottage all their lives. She felt that an undefined mystery hovered around their blighted lives. She knew, she says, that they were blighted, as the simplest child knows the withered leaf of November from the glowing green of May, and she questioned no more, half conscious that the mystery was sin and that knowledge of it would be sinful too.

But we turn from these sad pictures to brighter pages in the great books of human life. To Benjamin West saying: "My mother's kiss made me a painter." To John Randolph saying, "I should have been an atheist, if it had not been for one recollection, and that was the memory of the time when my departed mother used to take my little hands in hers and sank me on my knees to say: 'Our Father, who art in heaven.' Amid the cold of an Arctic expedition, Adam Isles found sickness had settled on part of his comrades, and the request came to him, "I think from one of the officers of the ship, saying: Isles, for God's sake, take some spirits, or we will be lost." Then the memory of the dear mother came back, and looking the entreaty in the face, he said, "I promised my mother I would not do it, and I wouldn't do it if I die in the ice."

I would ask, in conclusion, is there a branch of the human race in the Western Hemisphere which has greater need of the inspiring and uplifting influences that can flow out of the lives and examples of the truly enlightened than ourselves? Mothers who can teach their sons not to love pleasure or fear death; mothers who can teach their children to embrace every opportunity, employ every power, and use every means to build up a future to contrast with the old sad past. Men may boast of the aristocracy of blood; they may glory in the aristocracy of talent, and be proud of the aristocracy of wealth, but there is an aristocracy which must ever outrank them all, and that is the aristocracy of character.

The work of the mothers of our race is grandly constructive. It is for us to build above the wreck and ruin of the past more stately temples of thought and action. Some races have been overthrown, dashed in pieces, and destroyed but today the world is needing, fainting, for something better than the results of arrogance, aggressiveness, and indomitable power. We need mothers who are capable of being character builders, patient, loving, strong, and true, whose homes will be an uplifting power in the race. This is one of the greatest needs of the hour. No race can afford to neglect the enlightenment of its mothers. If you would have a clergy without virtue or morality, a manhood without honor, and a womanhood frivolous, mocking, and ignorant, neglect the education of your daughters. But if, on the other hand, you would have strong men, virtuous women, and good homes, then enlighten your women, so that they may be able to bless their homes by the purity of their lives, the tenderness of their hearts, and the strength of their intellects. From schools and colleges your children may come well versed in ancient lore and modern learning, but it is for us to learn and teach, within the shadow of our own homes, the highest and best of all sciences, the science of a true life. When the last lay of the minstrel shall die upon his ashy lips, and the sweetest numbers of the poet cease to charm his death-dulled ear; when the eye of the astronomer shall be too dim to mark the path of worlds that roll in light and power on high; and when all our earthly knowledge has performed for us its mission, and we are ready to lay aside our environments as garments we have outworn and outgrown if we have learned the science of a true life, we may rest assured that this acquirement will go with us through the valley and shadow of death, only to grow lighter and brighter through the eternities.

ATLANTA OFFERING

MY MOTHER'S KISSES

My mother's kiss, my mother's kiss,
I feel its impress now;
As in the bright and happy days
She pressed it on my brow.
You say it is a fancied thing
Within my memory fraught;
To me it has a sacred place—
The treasure house of thought.
Again, I feel her fingers glide
Amid my clustering hair;
I see the love-light in her eyes,
When all my life was fair.
Again, I hear her gentle voice
In warning or in love.
How precious was the faith that taught
My soul of things above.
The music of her voice is stilled,
Her lips are paled in death.
As precious pearls I'll clasp her words
Until my latest breath.
The world has scattered round my path
Honor and wealth and fame;
But naught so precious as the thoughts
That gather round her name.
And friends have placed upon my brow
The laurels of renown;
But she first taught me how to wear
My manhood as a crown.
My hair is silvered o'er with age,
I'm longing to depart;
To clasp again my mother's hand,
And be a child at heart.
To roam with her the glory-land
Where saints and angels greet;
To cast our crowns with songs of love
At our Redeemer's feet.

A Grain of Sand

Do you see this grain of sand
Lying loosely in my hand?
Do you know to me it brought
Just a simple loving thought?
When one gazes night by night
On the glorious stars of light,
Oh how little seems the span
Measured round the life of man.
Oh! how fleeting are his years
With their smiles and their tears;
Can it be that God does care
For such atoms as we are?
Then outspake this grain of sand
"I was fashioned by His hand
In the star lit realms of space
I was made to have a place."
"Should the ocean flood the world,
Were its mountains 'gainst me hurled,
All the force they could employ
Wouldn't a single grain destroy;
And if I, a thing so light,
Have a place within His sight;
You are linked unto his throne
Cannot live nor die alone.
In the everlasting arms
Mid life's dangers and alarms
Let calm trust your spirit fill;
Know He's God, and then be still."
Trustingly I raised my head
Hearing what the atom said;
Knowing man is greater far
Than the brightest sun or star.

THE CROCUSES

They heard the South wind sighing
A murmur of the rain;
And they knew that Earth was longing
To see them all again.
While the snow-drops still were sleeping
Beneath the silent sod;
They felt their new life pulsing
Within the dark, cold clod.
Not a daffodil nor daisy
Had dared to raise its head;
Not a fairhaired dandelion
Peeped timid from its bed;
Though a tremor of the winter
Did shivering through them run;
Yet they lifted up their foreheads
To greet the vernal sun.
And the sunbeams gave them welcome,
As did the morning air—
And scattered o'er their simple robes
Rich tints of beauty rare.
Soon a host of lovely flowers
From vales and woodland burst;
But in all that fair procession
The crocuses were first.
First to weave for Earth a chaplet
To crown her dear old head;
And to beautify the pathway
Where winter-still did tread.
And their loved and white haired mother
Smiled sweetly 'neath the touch,
When she knew her faithful children
Were loving her so much.

The Present Age

Say not the age is hard and cold—
I think it brave and grand;
When men of diverse sects and creeds
Are clasping hand in hand.
The Parsee from his sacred fires
Beside the Christian kneels;
And clearer light to Islam's eyes
The word of Christ reveals.
The Brahmin from his distant home
Brings thoughts of ancient lore;
The Bhuddist breaking bonds of caste
Divides mankind no more.
The meek-eyed sons of far Cathay
Are welcome round the board;
Not greed, nor malice drives away
These children of our Lord.
And Judah from whose trusted hands
Came oracles divine;
Now sits with those around whose hearts
The light of God doth shine.
Japan unbars her long sealed gates
From islands far away;
Her sons are lifting up their eyes
To greet the coming day.
The Indian child from forests wild
Has learned to read and pray;
The tomahawk and scalping knife
From him have passed away.
From centuries of servile toil
The Negro finds release,
And builds the fanes of prayer and praise
Unto the God of Peace.
England and Russia face to face
With Central Asia meet;
And on the far Pacific coast,

Chinese and natives greet.
Crusaders once with sword and shield
The Holy Land to save;
From Moslem hands did strive to clutch
The dear Redeemer's grave.
A battle greater, grander far
Is for the present age;
A crusade for the rights of man
To brighten history's page.
Where labor faints and bows her head,
And want consorts with crime;
Or men grown faithless sadly say
That evil is the time.
There is the field, the vantage ground
For every earnest heart;
To side with justice, truth and right
And act a noble part.
To save from ignorance and vice
The poorest, humblest child;
To make our age the fairest one
On which the sun has smiled;
To plant the roots of coming years
In mercy, love and truth;
And bid our weary, saddened earth
Again renew her youth.
Oh! earnest hearts! toil on in hope,
'Till darkness shrinks from light;
To fill the earth with peace and joy,
Let youth and age unite;
To stay the floods of sin and shame
That sweep from shore to shore;
And furl the banners stained with blood,
'Till war shall be no more.
Blame not the age, nor think it full
Of evil and unrest;
But say of every other age,
"This one shall be the best."
The age to brighten every path

By sin and sorrow trod;
For loving hearts to usher in
The commonwealth of God.

DEDICATION POEM

Dedication Poem on the reception of the annex to the home for aged colored people, from the bequest of Mr. Edward T. Parker.

Outcast from her home in Syria
In the lonely, dreary wild;
Heavy hearted, sorrow stricken,
Sat a mother and her child.
There was not a voice to cheer her
Not a soul to share her fate;
She was weary, he was fainting,—
And life seemed so desolate.
Far away in sunny Egypt
Was lone Hagar's native land;
Where the Nile in kingly bounty
Scatters bread throughout the land.
In the tents of princely Abram
She for years had found a home;
Till the stern decree of Sarah
Sent her forth the wild to roam.
Hour by hour she journeyed onward
From the shelter of their tent,
Till her footsteps slowly faltered
And the water all was spent;
Then she veiled her face in sorrow,
Feared her child would die of thirst;
Till her eyes with tears so holden
Saw a sparkling fountain burst.
Oh! how happy was that mother,
What a soothing of her pain;
When she saw her child reviving,
Life rejoicing through each vein
Does not life repeat this story,
Tell it over day by day?
Of the fountains of refreshment
Ever springing by our way.
Here is one by which we gather,

On this bright and happy day,
Just to bask beside a fountain
Making gladder life's highway.
Bringing unto hearts now aged
Who have borne life's burdens long,
Such a gift of love and mercy
As deserves our sweetest song.
Such a gift that even heaven
May rejoice with us below,
If the pure and holy angels
Join us in our joy and woe.
May the memory of the giver
In this home where age may rest,
Float like fragrance through the ages,
Ever blessing, ever blest.
When the gates of pearl are opened
May we there this friend behold,
Drink with him from living fountains,
Walk with him the streets of gold.
When life's shattered cords of music
Shall again be sweetly sung;
Then our hearts with life immortal,
Shall be young, forever young.

A Double Standard

Do you blame me that I loved him?
If when standing all alone
I cried for bread a careless world
Pressed to my lips a stone.
Do you blame me that I loved him,
That my heart beat glad and free,
When he told me in the sweetest tones
He loved but only me?
Can you blame me that I did not see
Beneath his burning kiss
The serpent's wiles, nor even hear
The deadly adder hiss?
Can you blame me that my heart grew cold
That the tempted, tempter turned;
When he was feted and caressed
And I was coldly spurned?
Would you blame him, when you draw from me
Your dainty robes aside,
If he with gilded baits should claim
Your fairest as his bride?
Would you blame the world if it should press
On him a civic crown;
And see me struggling in the depth
Then harshly press me down?
Crime has no sex and yet today
I wear the brand of shame;
Whilst he amid the gay and proud
Still bears an honored name.
Can you blame me if I've learned to think
Your hate of vice a sham,
When you so coldly crushed me down
And then excused the man?
Would you blame me if tomorrow
The coroner should say,
A wretched girl, outcast, forlorn,
Has thrown her life away?

Yes, blame me for my downward course,
But oh! remember well,
Within your homes you press the hand
That led me down to hell.
I'm glad God's ways are not our ways,
He does not see as man;
Within His love I know there's room
For those whom others ban.
I think before His great white throne,
His throne of spotless light,
That whited sepulchres shall wear
The hue-of endless night.
That I who fell, and he who sinned,
Shall reap as we have sown;
That each the burden of his loss
Must bear and bear alone.
No golden weights can turn the scale
Of justice in His sight;
And what is wrong in woman's life
In man's cannot be right.

The Dying Bondman

Life was trembling, faintly trembling
On the bondman's latest breath,
And he felt the chilling pressure
Of the cold, hard hand of Death.

He had been an African chieftain,
Worn his manhood as a crown;
But upon the field of battle
Had been fiercely stricken down.

He had longed to gain his freedom,
Waited, watched and hoped in vain,
Till his life was slowly ebbing—
Almost broken was his chain.

By his bedside stood the master,
Gazing on the dying one,
Knowing by the dull grey shadows
That life's sands were almost run.

"Master," said the dying bondman,
"Home and friends I soon shall see;
But before I reach my country,
Master write that I am free;"

"For the spirits of my fathers
Would shrink back from me in pride,
If I told them at our greeting
I a slave had lived and died;—"

"Give to me the precious token,
That my kindred dead may see—
Master! write it, write it quickly!
Master! write that I am free!"

At his earnest plea the master
Wrote for him the glad release,
O'er his wan and wasted features
Flitted one sweet smile of peace.

Eagerly he grasped the writing;
"I am free!" at last he said.
Backward fell upon the pillow,
He was free among the dead.

"A Little Child Shall Lead Them"

Only a little scrap of blue
Preserved with loving care,
But earth has not a brilliant hue
To me more bright and fair.
Strong drink, like a raging demon,
Laid on my heart his hand,
When my darling joined with others
The Loyal Legion band.
But mystic angels called away
My loved and precious child,
And o'er life's dark and stormy way
Swept waves of anguish wild.
This badge of the Loyal Legion
We placed upon her breast,
As she lay in her little coffin
Taking her last sweet rest.
To wear that badge as a token
She earnestly did crave,
So we laid it on her bosom
To wear it in the grave.
Where sorrow would never reach her
Nor harsh words smite her ear;
Nor her eyes in death dimmed slumber
Would ever shed a tear.
"What means this badge?" said her father,
Whom we had tried to save;
Who said, when we told her story,
"Don't put it in the grave."
We took the badge from her bosom
And laid it on a chair;
And men by drink deluded
Knelt by that badge in prayer.
And vowed in that hour of sorrow
From drink they would abstain;
And this little badge became the wedge
Which broke their galling chain.

FRANCES ELLEN WATKINS HARPER

And lifted the gloomy shadows
That overspread my life,
And flooding my home with gladness,
Made me a happy wife.
And this is why this scrap of blue
Is precious in my sight;
It changed my sad and gloomy home
From darkness into light.

The Sparrow's Fall

Too frail to soar—a feeble thing—
It fell to earth with fluttering wing;
But God, who watches over all,
Beheld that little sparrow's fall.
'Twas not a bird with plumage gay,
Filling the air with its morning lay;
'Twas not an eagle bold and strong,
Borne on the tempest's wing along.
Only a brown and weesome thing,
With drooping head and listless wing;
It could not drift beyond His sight
Who marshals the splendid stars of night.
Its dying chirp fell on His ears,
Who tunes the music of the spheres,
Who hears the hungry lion's call,
And spreads a table for us all.
Its mission of song at last is done,
No more will it greet the rising sun;
That tiny bird has found a rest
More calm than its mother's downy breast.
Oh, restless heart, learn thou to trust
In God, so tender, strong and just;
In whose love and mercy everywhere
His humblest children have a share.
If in love He numbers ev'ry hair,
Whether the strands be dark or fair,
Shall we not learn to calmly rest,
Like children, on our Father's breast?

FRANCES ELLEN WATKINS HARPER

God Bless Our Native Land

God bless our native land,
Land of the newly free,
Oh may she ever stand
For truth and liberty.
God bless our native land,
Where sleep our kindred dead,
Let peace at thy command
Above their graves be shed.
God help our native land,
Bring surcease to her strife,
And shower from thy hand
A more abundant life.
God bless our native land,
Her homes and children bless,
Oh may she ever stand
For truth and righteousness.

DANDELIONS

Welcome children of the Spring,
In your garbs of green and gold,
Lifting up your sun-crowned heads
On the verdant plain and wold.
As a bright and joyous troop
From the breast of earth ye came
Fair and lovely are your cheeks,
With sun-kisses all aflame.
In the dusty streets and lanes,
Where the lowly children play,
There as gentle friends ye smile,
Making brighter life's highway.
Dewdrops and the morning sun,
Weave your garments fair and bright,
And we welcome you today
As the children of the light.
Children of the earth and sun,
We are slow to understand
All the richness of the gifts
Flowing from our Father's hand.
Were our vision clearer far,
In this sin-dimmed world of ours,
Would we not more thankful be
For the love that sends us flowers?
Welcome, early visitants,
With your sun-crowned golden hair
With your message to our hearts
Of our Father's loving care.

The Building

"Build me a house," said the Master,
 "But not on the shifting sand,
 Mid the wreck and roar of tempests,
 A house that will firmly stand.
"I will bring thee windows of agates,
 And gates of carbuncles bright,
 And thy fairest courts and portals
 Shall be filled with love and light.
"Thou shalt build with fadeless rubies,
 All fashioned around the throne,
 A house that shall last forever,
 With Christ as the cornerstone.
"It shall be a royal mansion,
 A fair and beautiful thing,
 It will be the presence-chamber
 Of thy Saviour, Lord and King.
"Thy house shall be bound with pinions
 To mansions of rest above,
 But grace shall forge all the fetters
 With the links and cords of love.
"Thou shalt be free in this mansion
 From sorrow and pain of heart,
 For the peace of God shall enter,
 And never again depart."

Home, Sweet Home

Sharers of a common country,
They had met in deadly strife;
Men who should have been as brothers
Madly sought each other's life.
In the silence of the even,
When the cannon's lips were dumb,
'Thoughts of home and all its loved ones
To the soldier's heart would come.
On the margin of a river,
'Mid the evening's dews and damps,
Could be heard the sounds of music
Rising from two hostile camps.
One was singing of its section
Down in Dixie, Dixie's land,
And the other of the banner
Waved so long from strand to strand.
In the land where Dixie's ensign
Floated o'er the hopeful slave,
Rose the song that freedom's banner,
Starry-lighted, long might wave.
From the fields of strife and carnage,
Gentle thoughts began to roam,
And a tender strain of music
Rose with words of "Home, Sweet Home."
Then the hearts of strong men melted,
For amid our grief and sin
Still remains that "touch of nature,"
Telling us we all are kin.
In one grand but gentle chorus,
Floating to the starry dome,
Came the words that brought them nearer,
Words that told of "Home, Sweet Home."
For awhile, all strife forgotten,
They were only brothers then,
Joining in the sweet old chorus,
Not as soldiers, but as men.

FRANCES ELLEN WATKINS HARPER

Men whose hearts would flow together,
Though apart their feet might roam,
Found a tie they could not sever,
In the mem'ry of each home.
Never may the steps of carnage
Shake our land from shore to shore,
But may mother, home and Heaven,
Be our watchwords evermore.

The Pure in Heart Shall See God

They shall see Him in the crimson flush
Of morning's early light,
In the drapery of sunset,
Around the couch of night.
When the clouds drop down their fatness,
In late and early rain,
They shall see His glorious footprints
On valley, hill and plain.
They shall see Him when the cyclone
Breathes terror through the land;
They shall see Him 'mid the murmurs
Of zephyrs soft and bland.
They shall see Him when the lips of health,
Breath vigor through each nerve,
When pestilence clasps hands with death,
His purposes to serve.
They shall see Him when the trembling earth
Is rocking to and fro;
They shall see Him in the order
The seasons come and go.
They shall see Him when the storms of war
Sweep wildly through the land;
When peace descends like gentle dew
They still shall see His hand.
They shall see Him in the city
Of gems and pearls of light,
They shall see Him in his beauty,
And walk with Him in white.
To living founts their feet shall tend,
And Christ shall be their guide,
Beloved of God, their rest shall be
In safety by His side.

He "Had Not Where to Lay His Head"

The conies had their hiding-place,
The wily fox with stealthy tread
A covert found, but Christ, the Lord,
Had not a place to lay his head.
The eagle had an eyrie home,
The blithesome bird its quiet rest,
But not the humblest spot on earth
Was by the Son of God possessed.
Princes and kings had palaces,
With grandeur could adorn each tomb,
For Him who came with love and life,
They had no home, they gave no room.
The hands whose touch sent thrills of joy
Through nerves unstrung and palsied frame,
The feet that travelled for our need,
Were nailed unto the cross of shame.
How dare I murmur at my lot,
Or talk of sorrow, pain and loss,
When Christ was in a manger laid,
And died in anguish on the cross.
That homeless one beheld beyond
His lonely agonizing pain,
A love outflowing from His heart,
That all the wandering world would gain.

Go Work in My Vineyard

Go work in my vineyard, said the Lord,
And gather the bruised grain;
But the reapers had left the stubble bare,
And I trod the soil in pain.
The fields of my Lord are wide and broad,
He has pastures fair and green,
And vineyards that drink the golden light
Which flows from the sun's bright sheen.
I heard the joy of the reapers' song,
As they gathered golden grain;
Then wearily turned unto my task,
With a lonely sense of pain.
Sadly I turned from the sun's fierce glare.
And sought the quiet shade,
And over my dim and weary eyes
Sleep's peaceful fingers strayed.
I dreamed I joined with a restless throng,
Eager for pleasure and gain;
But ever and anon a stumbler fell,
And uttered a cry of pain.
But the eager crowd still hurried on,
Too busy to pause or heed,
When a voice rang sadly through my soul,
You must staunch these wounds that bleed.
My hands were weak, but I reached them out
To feebler ones than mine,
And over the shadows of my life
Stole the light of a peace divine.
Oh! then my task was a sacred thing,
How precious it grew in my eyes!
'Twas mine to gather the bruised grain
For the "Lord of Paradise."
And when the reapers shall lay their grain
On the floors of golden light,
I feel that mine with its broken sheaves
Shall be precious in His sight.

FRANCES ELLEN WATKINS HARPER

Though thorns may often pierce my feet,
And the shadows still abide,
The mists will vanish before His smile,
There will be light at eventide.

Renewal of Strength

The prison-house in which I live
Is falling to decay,
But God renews my spirit's strength,
Within these walls of clay.
For me a dimness slowly creeps
Around earth's fairest light,
But heaven grows clearer to my view,
And fairer to my sight.
It may be earth's sweet harmonies
Are duller to my ear,
But music from my Father's house
Begins to float more near.
Then let the pillars of my home
Crumble and fall away;
Lo, God's dear love within my soul
Renews it day by day.

FRANCES ELLEN WATKINS HARPER

JAMIE'S PUZZLE

There was grief within our household
Because of a vacant chair.
Our mother, so loved and precious,
No longer was sitting there.
Our hearts grew heavy with sorrow,
Our eyes with tears were blind,
And little Jamie was wondering,
Why we were left behind.
We had told our little darling,
Of the land of love and light,
Of the saints all crowned with glory,
And enrobed in spotless white.
We said that our precious mother,
Had gone to that land so fair,
To dwell with beautiful angels,
And to be forever there.
But the child was sorely puzzled,
Why dear grandmamma should go
To dwell in a stranger city,
When her children loved her so.
But again the mystic angel
Came with swift and silent tread,
And our sister, Jamie's mother,
Was enrolled among the dead.
To us the mystery deepened,
To Jamie it seemed more clear;
Grandma, he said, must be lonesome,
And mamma has gone to her.
But the question lies unanswered
In our little Jamie's mind,
Why she should go to our mother,
And leave her children behind;
To dwell in that lovely city,
From all that was dear to part,
From children who loved to nestle
So closely around her heart.

Dear child, like you, we are puzzled,
With problems that still remain;
But think in the great hereafter
Their meaning will all be plain.

Truth

A rock, for ages, stern and high,
Stood frowning 'gainst the earth and sky,
And never bowed his haughty crest
When angry storms around him prest.
Morn, springing from the arms of night,
Had often bathed his brow with light,
And kissed the shadows from his face
With tender love and gentle grace.
Day, pausing at the gates of rest,
Smiled on him from the distant West,
And from her throne the dark-browed Night
Threw round his path her softest light.
And yet he stood unmoved and proud,
Nor love, nor wrath, his spirit bowed;
He bared his brow to every blast
And scorned the tempest as it passed.
One day a tiny, humble seed—
The keenest eye would hardly heed—
Fell trembling at that stern rock's base,
And found a lowly hiding-place.
A ray of light, and drop of dew,
Came with a message, kind and true;
They told her of the world so bright,
Its love, its joy, and rosy light,
And lured her from her hiding-place,
To gaze upon earth's glorious face.
So, peeping timid from the ground,
She clasped the ancient rock around,
And climbing up with childish grace,
She held him with a close embrace;
Her clinging was a thing of dread;
Where'er she touched a fissure spread,
And he who'd breasted many a storm
Stood frowning there, a mangled-form;
A Truth, dropped in the silent earth,
May seem a thing of little worth,

'Till, spreading round some mighty wrong,
It saps its pillars proud and strong,
And o'er the fallen ruin weaves
The brightest blooms and fairest leaves.

Death of the Old Sea King

Twas a fearful night—the tempest raved
With loud and wrathful pride,
The storm-king harnessed his lightning steeds,
And rode on the raging tide.
The sea-king lay on his bed of death,
Pale mourners around him bent;
They knew the wild and fitful life
Of their chief was almost spent.
His ear was growing dull in death
When the angry storm he heard,
The sluggish blood in the old man's veins
With sudden vigor stirred.
"I hear them call," cried the dying man,
His eyes grew full of light;
"Now bring me here my warrior robes,
My sword and armor bright."
"In the tempest's lull I heard a voice,
I knew 'twas Odin's call.
The Valkyrs are gathering round my bed
To lead me unto his hall."
"Bear me unto my noblest ship,
Light up a funeral pyre;
I'll walk to the palace of the braves
Through a path of flame and fire."
Oh! wild and bright was the stormy light
That flashed from the old man's eye,
As they bore him from the couch of death
To his battle-ship to die,
And lit with many a mournful torch
The sea-king's dying bed,
And like a banner fair and bright
The flames around him spread.
But they heard no cry of anguish
Break through that fiery wall,
With rigid brow and silent lips
He was seeking Odin's hall.

Through a path of fearful splendor,
While strong men held their breath,
The brave old man went boldly forth
And calmly talked with death.

SAVE THE BOYS

Like Dives in the deeps of Hell
I cannot break this fearful spell,
Nor quench the fires I've madly nursed,
Nor cool this dreadful raging thirst.
Take back your pledge—ye come too late!
Ye cannot save me from my fate,
Nor bring me back departed joys;
But ye can try to save the boys.
Ye bid me break my fiery chain,
Arise and be a man again,
When every street with snares is spread,
And nets of sin where'er I tread.
No; I must reap as I did sow.
The seeds of sin bring crops of woe;
But with my latest breath I'll crave
That ye will try the boys to save.
These bloodshot eyes were once so bright;
This sin-crushed heart was glad and light;
But by the wine-cup's ruddy glow
I traced a path to shame and woe.
A captive to my galling chain,
I've tried to rise, but tried in vain—
The cup allures and then destroys.
Oh! from its thraldom save the boys.
Take from your streets those traps of hell
Into whose gilded snares I fell.
Oh! freemen, from these foul decoys
Arise, and vote to save the boys.
Oh, ye who license men to trade
In draughts that charm and then degrade,
Before ye hear the cry, Too late,
Oh, save the boys from my sad fate.

Nothing and Something

It is nothing to me, the beauty said,
With a careless toss of her pretty head;
The man is weak if he can't refrain
From the cup you say is fraught with pain.
It was something to her in after years,
When her eyes were drenched with burning tears,
And she watched in lonely grief and dread,
And startled to hear a staggering tread.

It is nothing to me, the mother said;
I have no fear that my boy will tread
In the downward path of sin and shame,
And crush my heart and darken his name.
It was something to her when that only son
From the path of right was early won,
And madly cast in the flowing bowl
A ruined body and sin-wrecked soul.

It is nothing to me, the young man cried:
In his eye was a flash of scorn and pride;
I heed not the dreadful things ye tell:
I can rule myself I know full well.
It was something to him when in prison he lay
The victim of drink, life ebbing away;
And thought of his wretched child and wife,
And the mournful wreck of his wasted life.

It is nothing to me, the merchant said,
As over his ledger he bent his head;
I'm busy today with tare and tret,
And I have no time to fume and fret.
It was something to him when over the wire
A message came from a funeral pyre—
A drunken conductor had wrecked a train,
And his wife and child were among the slain.

It is nothing to me, the voter said,
The party's loss is my greatest dread;
Then gave his vote for the liquor trade,
Though hearts were crushed and drunkards made.

It was something to him in after life,
When his daughter became a drunkard's wife
And her hungry children cried for bread,
And trembled to hear their father's tread.
Is it nothing for us to idly sleep
While the cohorts of death their vigils keep?
To gather the young and thoughtless in,
And grind in our midst a grist of sin?
It is something, yes, all, for us to stand
Clasping by faith our Saviour's hand;
To learn to labor, live and fight
On the side of God and changeless light.

VASHTI

She leaned her head upon her hand
And heard the King's decree—
"My lords are feasting in my halls;
Bid Vashti come to me.

"I've shown the treasures of my house,
My costly jewels rare,
But with the glory of her eyes
No rubies can compare.

"Adorn'd and crown'd I'd have her come,
With all her queenly grace,
And, 'mid my lords and mighty men,
Unveil her lovely face.

"Each gem that sparkles in my crown,
Or glitters on my throne,
Grows poor and pale when she appears,
My beautiful, my own!"

All waiting stood the chamberlains
To hear the Queen's reply.
They saw her cheek grow deathly pale,
But light flash'd to her eye:

"Go, tell the King," she proudly said,
"That I am Persia's Queen,
And by his crowds of merry men
I never will be seen.

"I'll take the crown from off my head
And tread it 'neath my feet,
Before their rude and careless gaze
My shrinking eyes shall meet.

"A queen unveil'd before the crowd!—
Upon each lip my name!—
Why, Persia's women all would blush
And weep for Vashti's shame!

"Go back!" she cried, and waved her hand,
And grief was in her eye:
"Go, tell the King," she sadly said,
"That I would rather die."

They brought her message to the King;
 Dark flash'd his angry eye;
 'Twas as the lightning ere the storm
 Hath swept in fury by.
 Then bitterly outspoke the King,
 Through purple lips of wrath—
"What shall be done to her who dares
 To cross your monarch's path?"
 Then spake his wily counsellors—
"O King of this fair land!
 From distant Ind to Ethiop,
 All bow to thy command.
"But if, before thy servants' eyes,
 This thing they plainly see,
 That Vashti doth not heed thy will
 Nor yield herself to thee,
"The women, restive 'neath our rule,
 Would learn to scorn our name,
 And from her deed to us would come
 Reproach and burning shame.
"Then, gracious King, sign with thy hand
 This stern but just decree,
 That Vashti lay aside her crown,
 Thy Queen no more to be."
 She heard again the King's command,
 And left her high estate;
 Strong in her earnest womanhood,
 She calmly met her fate,
 And left the palace of the King,
 Proud of her spotless name—
 A woman who could bend to grief,
 But would not bow to shame.

Thank God for Little Children

Thank God for little children,
Bright flowers by earth's wayside,
The dancing, joyous lifeboats
Upon life's stormy tide.
Thank God for little children;
When our skies are cold and gray,
They come as sunshine to our hearts,
And charm our cares away.
I almost think the angels,
Who tend life's garden fair,
Drop down the sweet wild blossoms
That bloom around us here.
It seems a breath of heaven
Round many a cradle lies,
And every little baby
Brings a message from the skies.
Dear mothers, guard these jewels,
As sacred offerings meet,
A wealth of household treasures
To lay at Jesus' feet.

The Martyr of Alabama

The following news item appeared in the newspapers throughout the country, issue of December 27th, 1894:

Tim Thompson, a little negro boy, was asked to dance for the amusement of some white toughs. He refused, saying he was a church member. One of the men knocked him down with a club and then danced upon his prostrate form. He then shot the boy in the hip. The boy is dead; his murderer is still at large.

He lifted up his pleading eyes,
And scanned each cruel face,
Where cold and brutal cowardice
Had left its evil trace.
It was when tender memories
Round Beth'lem's manger lay,
And mothers told their little ones
Of Jesu's natal day.
And of the Magi from the East
Who came their gifts to bring,
And bow in rev'rence at the feet
Of Salem's new-born King.
And how the herald angels sang
The choral song of peace,
That war should close his wrathful lips,
And strife and carnage cease.
At such an hour men well may hush
Their discord and their strife,
And o'er that manger clasp their hands
With gifts to brighten life.
Alas! that in our favored land,
That cruelty and crime
Should cast their shadows o'er a day,
The fairest pearl of time.
A dark-browed boy had drawn anear
A band of savage men,
Just as a hapless lamb might stray
Into a tiger's den.

Cruel and dull, they saw in him
For sport an evil chance,
And then demanded of the child
To give to them a dance.
"Come dance for us," the rough men said;
"I can't," the child replied,
"I cannot for the dear Lord's sake,
Who for my sins once died."
Tho' they were strong and he was weak,
He wouldn't his Lord deny.
His life lay in their cruel hands,
But he for Christ could die.
Heard they aright? Did that brave child
Their mandates dare resist?
Did he against their stern commands
Have courage to resist?
Then recklessly a man arose,
And dealt a fearful blow.
He crushed the portals of that life,
And laid the brave child low.
And trampled on his prostrate form,
As on a broken toy;
Then danced with careless, brutal feet,
Upon the murdered boy.
Christians! behold that martyred child!
His blood cries from the ground;
Before the sleepless eye of God,
He shows each gaping wound.
Oh! Church of Christ arise! arise!
Lest crimson stain thy hand,
When God shall inquisition make
For blood shed in the land.
Take sackcloth of the darkest hue,
And shroud the pulpits round;
Servants of him who cannot lie
Sit mourning on the ground.
Let holy horror blanch each brow,
Pale every cheek with fears,
And rocks and stones, if ye could speak,

FRANCES ELLEN WATKINS HARPER

Ye well might melt to tears.
Through every fane send forth a cry,
Of sorrow and regret,
Nor in an hour of careless ease
Thy brother's wrongs forget.
Veil not thine eyes, nor close thy lips,
Nor speak with bated breath;
This evil shall not always last,—
The end of it is death.
Avert the doom that crime must bring
Upon a guilty land;
Strong in the strength that God supplies,
For truth and justice stand.
For Christless men, with reckless hands,
Are sowing round thy path
The tempests wild that yet shall break
In whirlwinds of God's wrath.

The Night of Death

'Twas a night of dreadful horror,—
Death was sweeping through the land;
And the wings of dark destruction
Were outstretched from strand to strand.
Strong men's hearts grew faint with terror,
As the tempest and the waves
Wrecked their homes and swept them downward,
Suddenly to yawning graves.
'Mid the wastes of ruined households,
And the tempest's wild alarms,
Stood a terror-stricken mother
With a child within her arms.
Other children huddled 'round her,
Each one nestling in her heart;
Swift in thought and swift in action,
She at least from one must part.
Then she said unto her daughter,
"Strive to save one child from death."
"Which one?" said the anxious daughter,
As she stood with bated breath.
Oh! the anguish of that mother;
What despair was in her eye!
All her little ones were precious;
Which one should she leave to die?
Then outspake the brother Bennie:
"I will take the little one."
"No," exclaimed the anxious mother;
"No, my child, it can't be done."
"See! my boy, the waves are rising,
Save yourself and leave the child!"
"I will trust in Christ," he answered;
Grasped the little one and smiled.
Through the roar of wind and waters
Ever and anon she cried;
But throughout the night of terror
Never Bennie's voice replied.

FRANCES ELLEN WATKINS HARPER

But above the waves' wild surging
He had found a safe retreat,
As if God had sent an angel,
Just to guide his wandering feet.
When the storm had spent its fury,
And the sea gave up its dead,
She was mourning for her loved ones,
Lost amid that night of dread.
While her head was bowed in anguish,
On her ear there fell a voice,
Bringing surcease to her sorrow,
Bidding all her heart rejoice.
"Didn't I tell you true?" said Bennie,
And his eyes were full of light,
"When I told you God would help me
Through the dark and dreadful night?"
And he placed the little darling
Safe within his mother's arms,
Feeling Christ had been his guardian,
'Mid the dangers and alarms.
Oh! for faith so firm and precious,
In the darkest, saddest night,
Till life's gloom-encircled shadows
Fade in everlasting light.
And upon the mount of vision
We our loved and lost shall greet,
With earth's wildest storms behind us,
And its cares beneath our feet.

Mother's Treasures

Two little children sit by my side,
I call them Lily and Daffodil;
I gaze on them with a mother's pride,
One is Edna, the other is Will.
Both have eyes of starry light,
And laughing lips o'er teeth of pearl.
I would not change for a diadem
My noble boy and darling girl.
Tonight my heart o'erflows with joy;
I hold them as a sacred trust;
I fain would hide them in my heart,
Safe from tarnish of moth and rust.
What should I ask for my dear boy?
The richest gifts of wealth or fame?
What for my girl? A loving heart
And a fair and a spotless name?
What for my boy? That he should stand
A pillar of strength to the state?
What for my girl? That she should be
The friend of the poor and desolate?
I do not ask they shall never tread
With weary feet the paths of pain.
I ask that in the darkest hour
They may faithful and true remain.
I only ask their lives may be
Pure as gems in the gates of pearl,
Lives to brighten and bless the world—
This I ask for my boy and girl.
I ask to clasp their hands again
'Mid the holy hosts of heaven,
Enraptured say: "I am here, oh! God,
And the children Thou hast given."

The Refiner's Gold

He stood before my heart's closed door,
And asked to enter in;
But I had barred the passage o'er
By unbelief and sin.
He came with nail-prints in his hands,
To set my spirit free;
With wounded feet he trod a path
To come and sup with me.
He found me poor and brought me gold,
The fire of love had tried,
And garments whitened by his blood,
My wretchedness to hide.
The glare of life had dimmed my
Its glamour was too bright.
He came with ointment in his hands
To heal my darkened sight.
He knew my heart was tempest-tossed,
By care and pain oppressed;
He whispered to my burdened heart,
Come unto me and rest.
He found me weary, faint and worn,
On barren mountains cold;
With love's constraint he drew me on,
To shelter in his fold.
Oh! foolish heart, how slow wert thou
To welcome thy dear guest,
To change thy weariness and care
For comfort, peace and rest.
Close to his side, oh! may I stay,
Just to behold his face,
Till I shall wear within my soul
The image of his grace.
The grace that changes hearts of stone
To tenderness and love,
And bids us run with willing feet
Unto his courts above.

A Story of Rebellion

The treacherous sands had caught our boat,
And held it with a strong embrace
And death at our imprisoned crew
Was sternly looking face to face.
With anxious hearts, but failing strength,
We strove to push the boat from shore;
But all in vain, for there we lay
With bated breath and useless oar.
Around us in a fearful storm
The fiery hail fell thick and fast;
And we engirded by the sand,
Could not return the dreadful blast.
When one arose upon whose brow
The ardent sun had left his trace;
A noble purpose strong and high
Uplighting all his dusky face.
Perchance within that fateful hour
The wrongs of ages thronged apace;
But with it came the glorious hope
Of swift deliverance to his race.
Of galling chains asunder rent,
Of severed hearts again made one,
Of freedom crowning all the land
Through battles gained and victories won.
"Some one," our hero firmly said,
"Must die to get us out of this;"
Then leaped upon the strand and bared
His bosom to the bullets' hiss.
"But ye are soldiers, and can fight,
May win in battles yet unfought;
I have no offering but my life,
And if they kill me it is nought."
With steady hands he grasped the boat,
And boldly pushed it from the shore;
Then fell by rebel bullets pierced,
His life work grandly, nobly o'er.

Our boat was rescued from the sands
And launched in safety on the tide;
But he our comrade good and grand,
In our defence had bravely died.

Burial of Sarah

He stood before the sons of Heth,
  And bowed his sorrowing head;
"I've come," he said, "to buy a place
  Where I may lay my dead."
"I am a stranger in your land,
  My home has lost its light;
  Grant me a place where I may lay
  My dead away from sight."
Then tenderly the sons of Heth
  Gazed on the mourner's face,
  And said, "Oh, Prince, amid our dead,
  Choose thou her resting-place."
"The sepulchres of those we love,
  We place at thy command;
  Against the plea thy grief hath made
  We close not heart nor hand."
The patriarch rose and bowed his head,
  And said, "One place I crave;
  'Tis at the end of Ephron's field,
  And called Machpelah's cave."
"Entreat him that he sell to me
  For her last sleep that cave;
  I do not ask for her I loved
  The freedom of a grave."
  The son of Zohar answered him,
  "Hearken, my lord, to me;
  Before our sons, the field and cave
  I freely give to thee."
"I will not take it as a gift,"
  The grand old man then said;
"I pray thee let me buy the place
  Where I may lay my dead."
  And with the promise in his heart,
  His seed should own that land,
  He gave the shekels for the field
  He took from Ephron's hand.

FRANCES ELLEN WATKINS HARPER

And saw afar the glorious day
tis chosen seed should tread,
The soil where he in sorrow lay
His loved and cherished dead.

GOING FAST

She came from the East a fair, young bride,
With a light and a bounding heart,
To find in the distant West a home
With her husband to make a start.
He builded his cabin far away,
Where the prairie flower bloomed wild;
Her love made lighter all his toil,
And joy and hope around him smiled.
She plied her hands to life's homely tasks,
And helped to build his fortunes up;
While joy and grief, like bitter and sweet,
Were mingled and mixed in her cup.
He sowed in his fields of golden grain,
All the strength of his manly prime;
Nor music of birds, nor brooks, nor bees,
Was as sweet as the dollar's chime.
She toiled and waited through weary years
For the fortune that came at length;
But toil and care and hope deferred,
Had stolen and wasted her strength.
The cabin changed to a stately home,
Rich carpets were hushing her tread;
But light was fading from her eye,
And the bloom from her cheek had fled.
Her husband was adding field to field,
And new wealth to his golden store;
And little thought the shadow of death
Was entering in at his door.
Slower and heavier grew her step,
While his gold and his gains increased;
But his proud domain had not the charm
Of her humble home in the East.
He had no line to sound the depths
Of her tears repressed and unshed;
Nor dreamed 'mid plenty a human heart
Could be starving, but not for bread.

FRANCES ELLEN WATKINS HARPER

Within her eye was a restless light,
And a yearning that never ceased,
A longing to see the dear old home
She had left in the distant East.
A longing to clasp her mother's hand,
And nestle close to her heart,
And to feel the heavy cares of life
Like the sun-kissed shadows depart.
The hungry heart was stilled at last;
Its restless, baffled yearning ceased.
A lonely man sat by the bier
Of a corpse that was going East.

The Hermit's Sacrifice

From Rome's palaces and villas
Gaily issued forth a throng;
From her humbler habitations
Moved a human tide along.
Haughty dames and blooming maidens,
Men who knew not mercy's sway,
Thronged into the Coliseum
On that Roman holiday.
From the lonely wilds of Asia,
From her jungles far away,
From the distant torrid regions,
Rome had gathered beasts of prey.
Lions restless, roaring, rampant,
Tigers with their stealthy tread,
Leopards bright, and fierce, and fiery,
Met in conflict wild and dread.
Fierce and fearful was the carnage
Of the maddened beasts of prey,
As they fought and rent each other
Urged by men more fierce than they.
Till like muffled thunders breaking
On a vast and distant shore,
Fainter grew the yells of tigers,
And the lions' dreadful roar.
On the crimson-stained arena
Lay the victims of the fight;
Eyes which once had glared with anguish,
Lost in death their baleful light.
Then uprose the gladiators
Armed for conflict unto death,
Waiting for the prefect's signal,
Cold and stern with bated breath.
"Ave Caesar, morituri,
Te, salutant," rose the cry
From the lips of men ill-fated,
Doomed to suffer and to die.

Then began the dreadful contest,
 Lives like chaff were thrown away,
 Rome with all her pride and power
 Butchered for a holiday.
 Eagerly the crowd were waiting,
 Loud the clashing sabres rang,
 When between the gladiators
 All unarmed a hermit sprang.
"Cease your bloodshed," cried the hermit,
"On this carnage place your ban;"
 But with flashing swords they answered,
"Back unto your place, old man."
 From their path the gladiators
 Thrust the strange intruder back,
 Who between their hosts advancing
 Calmly parried their attack.
 All undaunted by their weapons,
 Stood the old heroic man;
 While a maddened cry of anger
 Through the vast assembly ran.
"Down with him," cried out the people,
 As with thumbs unbent they glared,
 Till the prefect gave the signal
 That his life should not be spared.
 Men grew wild with wrathful passion,
 When his fearless words were said
 Cruelly they fiercely showered
 Stones on his devoted head.
 Bruised and bleeding fell the hermit,
 Victor in that hour of strife;
 Gaining in his death a triumph
 That he could not win in life.
 Had he uttered on the forum
 Struggling thoughts within him born,
 Men had jeered his words as madness,
 But his deed they could not scorn.
 Not in vain had been his courage,
 Nor for naught his daring deed;
 From his grave his mangled body

Did for wretched captives plead.
From that hour Rome, grown more thoughtful,
Ceased her sport in human gore;
And into her Coliseum
Gladiators came no more.

Songs for the People

Let me make the songs for the people,
Songs for the old and young;
Songs to stir like a battle-cry
Wherever they are sung.
Not for the clashing of sabres,
For carnage nor for strife;
But songs to thrill the hearts of men
With more abundant life.
Let me make the songs for the weary,
Amid life's fever and fret,
Till hearts shall relax their tension,
And careworn brows forget.
Let me sing for little children,
Before their footsteps stray,
Sweet anthems of love and duty,
To float o'er life's highway.
I would sing for the poor and aged,
When shadows dim their sight;
Of the bright and restful mansions,
Where there shall be no night.
Our world, so worn and weary,
Needs music, pure and strong,
To hush the jangle and discords
Of sorrow, pain, and wrong.
Music to soothe all its sorrow,
Till war and crime shall cease;
And the hearts of men grown tender
Girdle the world with peace.

A Note About the Author

Frances Ellen Watkins Harper (1825–1911) was an African American abolitionist, suffragist, poet, and novelist. Born free in Baltimore, Maryland, Harper became one of the first women of color to publish a work of literature in the United States when her debut poetry collection *Forest Leaves* appeared in 1845. In 1850, she began to teach sewing at Union Seminary in Columbus, Ohio. The following year, alongside chairman of the Pennsylvania Abolition Society William Still, she began working as an abolitionist in earnest, helping slaves escape to Canada along the Underground Railroad. In 1854, having established herself as a prominent public speaker and political activist, Harper published *Poems on Miscellaneous Subjects*, a resounding critical and commercial success. Over the course of her life, Harper founded and participated in several progressive organizations, including the Women's Christian Temperance Union and the National Association of Colored Women. At the age of sixty-seven, Harper published *Iola Leroy, or Shadows Uplifted*, becoming one of the first African American women to publish a novel.

A Note from the Publisher

Spanning many genres, from non-fiction essays to literature classics to children's books and lyric poetry, Mint Edition books showcase the master works of our time in a modern new package. The text is freshly typeset, is clean and easy to read, and features a new note about the author in each volume. Many books also include exclusive new introductory material. Every book boasts a striking new cover, which makes it as appropriate for collecting as it is for gift giving. Mint Edition books are only printed when a reader orders them, so natural resources are not wasted. We're proud that our books are never manufactured in excess and exist only in the exact quantity they need to be read and enjoyed.

Discover more of your favorite
classics with Bookfinity™.

- Track your reading with custom book lists.
- Get great book recommendations for your
  personalized Reader Type.
- Add reviews for your favorite books.
- AND MUCH MORE!

Visit **bookfinity.com** and take the fun
Reader Type quiz to get started.

Enjoy our classic and modern companion pairings!

Printed in the USA
CPSIA information can be obtained
at www.ICGtesting.com
LVHW041814090923
757656LV00002B/129